Keeping Your Toddler on Track till Mommy Gets Back

The Toddler Survival Guide
for
21st Century Dads

also from
clearing skies press

*Keeping the Baby Alive
till Your Wife Gets Home*

. . . .

upcoming from
clearing skies press

*Keeping Your Grandchild Alive
till His Ungrateful Parents Get Back*

visit us online

clearingskies.com

Keeping Your Toddler on Track till Mommy Gets Back

⌐   ⌐   ⌐   ⌐   ⌐   ⌐   ⌐

The Toddler Survival Guide
for
21st Century Dads

by
Walter Roark

Cover illustration by Jason Snape
Interior illustrations by Jason Snape and Meghan Roark

clearing skies press

Greg,
Best always
to you, Lisa and
the Kids.
Skeeter
5-11-04

a clearing skies press original, First Edition. April, 2003.
Copyright © 2003 by Walter Roark

Clearing Skies Press   4002 Dunbarton Way   Roswell, GA 30075
770-518-8931   visit us @ clearingskies.com

ISBN 0-9707937-1-5

. . . .

. . . .

Publisher's Cataloging-in-Publication Data:

Roark, Walter.
    Keeping your toddler on track till mommy gets back :
the toddler survival guide for 21st century dads / by Walter Roark.
--1st ed.
 p. cm.

1. Toddlers.   2. Child rearing—Humor.
3. Fatherhood—Popular works.   4. Father and toddler.   I. Title

HQ774.R63 2003   649'.122—dc21

10 9 8 7 6 5 4 3 2 1

Despite every effort to furnish the reader with precise, authoritative, indispensible information, the publisher and author accept no responsibility whatever for any type of toddler disaster, natural or unnatural, as well as physical damage, and/or loss of paternal self-esteem caused by any toddler, especially one who hasn't taken time to read the content herein.

Dedication

Thank you, Susan, for helping
make all things possible on the road of life;
and a special thank you for conspiring with
our children to drive me crazy
long before we reach the end of the road

⌐   ⌐   ⌐   ⌐   ⌐   ⌐   ⌐

Mental wounds not healing
Who and what's to blame
I'm going off the rails on a crazy train

—Ozzy Osbourne

Table of Contents

Chapter three

The Toddler Table: Serving Whine with Every Meal

•What's Eating Your Toddler   •Dad's Bad Day at the Toddler Cafe—*Oral Exam*   •Down the Hatch and Happy •Your Toddler Doesn't Know Beans

Chapter four

Temper Tantrum: The Toddler National Anthem

•Newton's Laws of the Toddler Tantrum   •The Sum of All Tantrums   •Tantrum Trouble Dead Ahead •Begging for Trouble with Rewards and Ransoms •The Ten Commandments of Toddler Tantrums

Chapter five

How Not to be a Weenie When It's Time to Wean

•Exploring the *Great Milky Way*   •A Subject Close to Your Wife's Heart   •Nipping Nipples in the Bud, Bud •Pop Quiz for Crusading Weenies, Weaners and Winners

Chapter nine

Chapter ten

Bibliography: Pop and Todd's Top 40 Toddlerific Hits

The Terror of Toddler Care

from a dad who's been there—
and survived every toddler trick in the book
(including this book)

an introduction

⌐ ⌐ ⌐ ⌐ ⌐ ⌐ ⌐

Think about a simple comparison of babies and toddlers. They're both lovable little people who require a lot of care. Either way, you need a vast reservoir of parenting skill, quick-witted reactions and superior decision-making ability. And that only gets you to square one.

The second you're squatting on square one, with your head in your hands looking for answers, some (tiny) body puts a move on you, slips out of sight and you're suddenly a pawn in a scary game of *Toddler Hide-and-Seek*.

[1]

Okay. Like we might in a good chess match, let's step away from the board a minute and apply a good dose of logic to the situation, from a masculine point of view. Together, let's size it up right.

Compared to when he was a baby, your toddler is bigger, faster, smarter, and of course, older. You're older too. You might even be bigger as well—check in the mirror and see if it's true. But chances are, you're not quite as fast as you used to be. And whether you think you're smart or not, you have no chance to match your toddler's amazing way of learning new stuff every minute of every day.

Who do you turn to? What does a Dad do? How can you catch up with your tricky offspring's learning curve?

Over a quiet, rare, candle-glow dinner-for-two you could ask your wife to spoil the occasion, stop enjoying her meal, then spend the next four hours and 45 minutes explaining to you what taking care of toddlers is all about.

But you're probably like me. You're a reader and a self-sufficient type, and you might decide to do a goodly amount of research with a few serious toddler care books. (Thankfully, the one you're reading can't be taken too seriously.) I asked my wife about this approach and she walked back from the bookshelf with a fiendish grin on her face, lugging a gargantuan, crazy-thick book in both hands. She promptly dropped it in my lap.

I'm not sure what she expected, but the impact of this five-pound book on my crotch may prevent us from ever expecting children again.

She expected me to read it, and I expected I would read it, but it was bigger than *War and Peace* and fatter than *Atlas Shrugged*. Before getting through the first chapter, I expect I was suffering from deadly information overload.

Frankly, Bob, Joe and Ted, I yearned for something slimmer. To the point. Something really honest. A book without the fuzzy feel-good tips women love to write about. A book about toddlers written by a man who understands some of the feelings men have about the little beings we help create.

This is the book.

First, this book states plainly that it is a scary responsibility taking good care of your toddler. But you have weapons to combat the fear. You're alert and aware and you have touch, taste, hearing, seeing and a sense of smell—five valuable, fully activated detection devices to use on-duty every day. Till his faculties improve, your toddler can only use one or two of these at a time.

But listen up, you have two additional senses that are even more precious.

COMMON SENSE

And the most priceless of all,

A SENSE OF HUMOR

Yet, if you could only take one with you when you ride into Toddlerville, I'd take the second.

That's what this book is all about.

⌐ ⌐ ⌐ ⌐ ⌐

The Terrible Twos

the real truth—and it ain't exactly news

a prologue

⌐   ⌐   ⌐   ⌐   ⌐   ⌐   ⌐

Your sweet baby has been working toward toddlerhood since birth. As a dedicated, doting, do-gooding Dad, you've made a good-faith attempt to work with Baby on getting to toddlerhood in one piece. Someone may have suffered a few wounds along the way—a knock here, a scratch there, and even recently, a bad fall and a purple bruise that took weeks to heal. And we're just talking about whacks to your ego, not Baby's physical mishaps.

So as the paternal heads of the clan (battered noggins or not) we have to ask ourselves one logical question at the beginning of this journey into the Land of Toddlers. That's right, before you and I take a seat on this wild-and-wooly roller coaster ride through the 'hood where toddlers hang, we need to know one thing: *When is a Toddler officially a Toddler? And does it really matter?*

Many (mostly female) experts decree that your precious babe gets his or her diploma and arrives at Toddler U the minute the clock strikes 13 months. Or 15 months. Or 18 months. But guess what? It ain't necessarily so.

Babies and toddlers have growth spurts (just like teenagers, see Chapter 9), and they can spurt anytime. When you least suspect it, your babykums will bust through three sizes of coveralls in four months flat. And every kid grows at a different rate. So don't worry your legendary paternal pride about how he/she compares with the kid across the street. Every body's different.

Honestly, I don't think anybody can say when your baby turns toddler. But I think they lumped the terms "Toddlers" and "Terrible Twos" together for a reason. Two seems to be the key here. For example, when all's said and done, your toddler only needs two traits to be labeled a true TODD or TODDETTE. He or she has to

1. WALK
on two feet, all of the time, regardless of how many stumbles, splits or splats happen in a 24-hour period

[6]

2. TALK
at least a few words you can actually understand—
NO! GIMME! I WANNA! MINE! and MOMMY!
don't count. Of course, DADDY! does

Naturally you can christen your babette with the toddler label any time you like. After all, you're the doggone
Daddy and you can most likely tell a toddler when you see
one. (But as the old saying goes, you probably won't be able
to tell 'em much!)

Me, I put two and two together and came up with two
years/24 months as a starting point for the grand exploration
of toddlerdom. It seems sensible. After all, if we fathers don't
know best, we can at least trust our favorite department store.
There the racks sport infant sizes like 0-3 Months, 6-9 Months
and 12-24 months. For Toddlers, logically, they have 2-4T.
And department stores have been in this business a lot longer
than you and I.

But since every toddler travels on her own timetable,
I'd start looking out for true toddler traits from about 15
months on. That way, you won't be caught by surprise—even
if you can't catch your toddler.

So it's the two of you, you and your 18- to 24-month-
old (or close enough) saying bye-bye to simple times and all
things Baby—and hello to the complicated, weird but wonderful, carnival-like state of toddlerhood. It's a hoot. Like a
man who wandered into a freak show tent, you'll be seeing,
hearing and smelling very odd things all around you during
toddler times.

For example, your delightful two-year-old may decide suddenly to drop down on the supermarket floor and pitch what my mother used to call a full-blown Kyniption fit. You'll see the bag of potato chips hit the floor, witness the stomping, then hear the crunching and the screeching. As you reach down to help up your former baby who's screaming, toddler-like, "TATO! TATO! TATO!", you pick him/her up and feel the instant silence and smell the puke as well as the poop.

What are you going to do now? Be a *BABY* about it?

To borrow one of Todd's favorite words..."NO!"

You've read *Keeping Your Toddler on Track till Mommy Gets Back*. You're in-tune with the toddler mind. You're in perfect harmony whatever the pitch, Kyniption fit or not. You're not going to let the Terrible Twos give you a bad attitude. Even though every mother up and down the aisle is staring at you, waiting for you to crack—you're going to be as cool as the frozen waffles in your cart.

You'll reach into your toddler bag, pull out one of your favorite, giant-sized moist towelettes and wipe the hurl off Todd's chin. Then you'll strap a sturdy rubber band to each of his overall legs, below the knee. With the up-chuck cleared and the stool contained, you'll head to the Express Lane with an air of total confidence.

And even though you'll know deep-down that the toddler years really are terrible, you won't be showing a single soul. Through the stench and the nausea, you'll be smiling at the stares, laughing at the cashier and skipping all the way to your car.

[8]

And when you walk in the door hand-in-hand, oozing poop, your wife will ask, "How did you and Todd do at the grocery store?"

You'll pat Todd's head, reach in the grocery bag, pull out a rotten piece of fruit covered with slobber and puke, and say, "Just peachy, darling. Would you like to hear our version of the *Toddler National Anthem*—in two-part harmony?"

2-for-1 Tantrums on Aisle Eight

Keeping Your Toddler on Track till Mommy Gets Back

The Toddler Survival Guide for 21st Century Dads

Walter Roark

Chapter one

Too Pooped
to Pop

*What we have here, gentlemen,
is a disaster in the making...
failure to communicate
coupled with a two-way energy crisis*

Many people tend to confuse the message a celebrated sociologist had in mind when she coined the term, "nuclear family." Academicians define "nuclear" family as a husband, wife and their children; the core being the couple, with offspring following.

That sounds fine. Until you read between the lines.

Parents who have youngsters that happen to be wild-eyed, totally-energized toddlers recognize a different, much more disturbing definition of the term *nuclear*.

[13]

The Meltdown
of Parental Authority

Look at that innocent face. Hard to believe that the main thing he or she's learning to do is manipulate you. Like a little nuclear reactor on wheels, unstable yet brilliant, your sweet baby is learning unhealthy secrets about how to fuel a reaction and rule your household. Bubbling over with energy and radiating confidence, your offspring is quickly acquiring the power to blacken your day or brighten your night. Depending on his or her mood.

And you thought you were in charge? Who do you think you are, Mommy?

Let's hope not. Everyone has to have an identity. Yours is Daddy. So take a minute. Put on your feeding apron and look in the mirror.

Repeat three times,
"I may not be Mommy, but I'm still important..."

Then repeat another three times,
"I am a man, but I can do everything Mommy does... and I do look good in an apron."

Now, get back in the breakfast nook and serve your toddler his perfectly browned tater tots before he/she screams for the female side of the parenting crew.

[14]

Later, if you have time, you can ask yourself two heart-to-heart questions.

Question One: "Can I really do everything Mommy does?" The answer? YES...except for breastfeeding. Or at least you haven't been allowed to for a long time. Hopefully soon you will regain your special place close to your loved one's heart.

Question Two: "But can I do everything as well as Mommy?" The answer? NO. But that doesn't mean you should stop trying. Keep wearing the apron, keep singing the lullabies, keep wiping the hiney. Keep thinking less like a man, more like a Mommy. It takes time.

The only trouble is, most of the time, you won't have time to think. When you're on Toddler-Daddy-duty, you'll be dealing with one disaster after another. Your Todd or Toddette is going to keep you so busy all of your neurons will be tied up in knots. Your brain will swell from decision-making overload.

Feed...Now?   Poop...Where?   Scream...What? Bite...Who?   Hit...Head?   Poke...Eye?   Laugh...Why? Wail...Spank?   Bug...Eat?   Feed...Still?

Oh, Baby! If you could just wire up an off-switch and strap it between your son's shoulder blades. Then when your former babykin's explodes with bad behavior and abusive babble just before dinner... when he shares a bug with the sweet toddlerette from next door before slapping her over the head with a fly swatter—you could reach down, turn him off, then calmly pick up his wailing playmate and apologize.

Instead of flailing arms and bloodcurdling, jealous screams, wouldn't it be delicious to look down at little Jack's motionless body and vacant stare and say, "Sorry, old Buddy, we've reached maximum overload and I had to shut you down. As soon as you cool off, I'll put you back online.

"Meanwhile, let's all enjoy a little bonus serving of peace and quiet at the dinner table. We'll keep yours warm...*Bon Appetit!*"

The Core of the Problem

The main thing is, you can't afford to blow your top, Pop. The first and last thing all we dads should remember is that every ounce of a toddler's energy is hot-wired to getting what he wants—NOW! Your toddler's concept of time is about the size of an atom. And he or she has no concept whatsoever about sharing.

You've got the right formula alright if you've figured out that S-H-A-R-I-N-G is the key missing element in a toddler's lifestyle. When toddlers get together socially, sharing ain't listed on the agenda. It's a no-show. A drop-out. A no-go. You can talk about it all you want, but trust me, nobody's listening.

You can do demonstrations. You can jump on the coffee table and do pantomime. You can put together a state-of-the-art multimedia computer show to wow your non-sharing toddler crowd. You can SHOUT out the SH-word's virtue. You can SHIFT and SHAKE and SHIMMY with the SH-word tattooed across your chest.

[16]

Code Red Shutdown

As a last resort (pun intended), you can roll the video camera and pretend you're reenacting a scene from the movie, The S-H-I-N-I-N-G. *A la* Jack Nicholson, you can brandish a playschool broom like an ax, shout, "Here's Daddy!" and try to scare your toddler audience into S-H-A-R-I-N-G. That won't work either.

When the audience boos you off the stage, you'll be tempted to share a shorter SH-word with them. Don't do it. That's a SH-word toddlers remember. Everyone will know the source when the same word comes out of your toddler's mouth. At that point you will be in deep...well, doo-doo. In fact, remember Doo-Doo and forget the SH-word. You'll go far in Toddlerville using disgusting and/or goofball-type words such as No-No, Uh-Oh, Yum-Yum, Boo-Boo, Doo-Doo, Boogey, Tee-Tee, Poo-Poo and Pee-Pee. Don't worry about sounding stupid, your wife and baby sitter will think it's cute. The short SH-word is not cute. You will not be well-liked in Toddlerville using any type of SH-word.

So your roly-poly, cute-as-a-button Baby is turning toddler whether you like it or not. You've finally recognized the core of the problem. You've given up trying to teach S-H-A-R-E to an audience with selective hearing. But are you still having trouble keeping up with the changes? Are you feeling dead-tired—but your little buddy has unlimited energy? Do you sense parental and paternal authority slipping away?

You need to get in shape now. After all, it's a long haul to the other side of Toddlerhood. What you need is a good probe of your prime-time toddler perception. You need to tally up how you rank compared to other disaster victims just like you.

Partner in crime, you've come to the right place. On this test of your Poppa-aptitude, all you need to post a good score is a double-dose of good sense. Namely, your sense of logic and your sense of humor.

Good luck, brother.

Pop's Unique-to-Toddlers/ Disaster Aptitude Test (P.U.T./D.A.T.)

We named it the "Put Dat" drill, because fathers spend so much time saying to their toddlers, *"Put dat down!"* and *"Put dat away!"* and especially, *"Don't put dat in your mouth!"*

Before you start the disaster drill, make a pledge to yourself to be honest to your offspring and your spouse by not cheating. This is a simple TRUE-FALSE quiz and that means you should stand a good chance of getting half the answers right just by guessing. Of course I didn't, but it's because my wife tricked me. She distracted me by saying things like, "Oh, c'mon. you know the answer to *this* one."

I know you can do better than I did. Consider a do-it-yourself testing procedure, then your wife won't even have to be involved. But after you get started, if your masculine competitiveness gets the best of you, and you catch yourself glancing for the answer before thinking about it, just place a bookmark below as you read each question.

TAKING THE P.U.T./D.A.T.

Give each of these ten drills your full intelligence as you prepare for a special breed of toddler-disaster soon to plague your glitch-free, happy-go-lucky lifestyle. Don't be a baby. Put your hard-hat on and dig in...

<u>Uh-Oh 1</u>: You should assume everything is going dandy when, with his back to you, your 20-month son plays quietly in the corner with a tennis ball while you linger over the automobile classifieds.

True or False?

Answer: *False.* No child at this age sits still that long unless you're reading the *Weekly Neighbor* with a single page of car ads. He may have been kidnapped and replaced with a blow-up doll, or he may be overcome by dog germs from the tennis ball. Check him out—quickly!

<u>Uh-Oh 2</u>: The first time your wife comes home with a size 2T polo shirt from Macy's, you'll know your son is a bona fide toddler—a true disaster waiting to happen.

True or False?

Answer: *False.* Toddlers don't wait for parents' approval or involvement o turn overnight from sweet babies to evil little humans. Beware and be ready.

[20]

Uh-Oh 3: You should be careful—and expect anything—when you invite over important people, like your boss, to meet your lovely 30-month-old daughter.

True or False?

Answer: *True*. After Mr. Brice leans down and your charming toddler gives him a peck on the cheek, you might fool yourself into thinking your dreams about a smooth greeting have come true. Then when he's leaving and walking out the door you'll hear, "Daddy, dat your Doo-Doo Head boss? Doo-Doo Head go now? Bye, Doo-Doo Head!"

Uh-Oh 4: Every time your wife is at a sales seminar or other business function you should make it a point to ring her cel phone on the quarter-hour to tell her how much you love caring for your precious toddler.

True or False?

Answer: *False*. Do you want her to call you when you escape to the golf course? Are you a moron? Besides, you need to save your lies for more important situations.

Uh-Oh 5: In nice weather you've discovered your 25-month-old son will spend hours in the sandbox playing happily. The best way to share his joy is to join him.

True or False?

Answer: *False*. With toddlers, it's always wise to remember the saying, "*Let Sleeping Dogs Lie*." So if they're happy, don't wake them from this random moment of bliss. Besides, if he thinks you're trying to share something other than his joy—like his bucket, for example— he'll probably stab you in the toe with his shovel.

Uh-Oh 6: As a loving father, you're simply desperate to teach your toddler-daughter how to share. That's why you should offer her your La-Z-Boy recliner, your bowling ball and a box of premium cigars, then take her for a rockin', rollin', smokin' good time on the riding mower.

True or False?

Answer: *True*. If you can't swing a night out with the guys at the Brunswick Lanes, this could be the next best thing. Of course, your wife might start proceedings to have you put away. But you and your daughter will have loads of fun—and share some wacky memories in the meantime. Just keep the cigar smoke and exhaust fumes to a minimum.

Uh-Oh 7: You're tuckered out at the end of a long weekend with your wife away on business—you just want to finish the Sunday sports section. This is the perfect time to let Todd, almost three, stretch his legs (and independence) by walking the dog alone in the park.

True or False?

Answer: *True.* for Toy Poodle, Chihuahua, Pekingese or Terrier. *False* for Great Dane, Chow, Wolfhound or Labrador. But if you really want to make Todd feel like a big boy, how about hopping in his little red wagon and having him pull you around the park while you catch up on the hockey news?

<u>Uh-Oh 8</u>: You smell a rat when your 34-month-old sweetie-pie giggles, tugs at your sleeve and requests a different bedtime story, after she's demanded the same Mother Goose tale 34 nights in a row. Based on your intuition, you should ask her why she's changed her mind.

True or False?

Answer: *False.* This one's simple. You should know by now, for heaven's sake, that you NEVER ask a female why she's changed her mind. That's her business. And what makes you think you have intuition? Speaking of business, that's most likely a big B.M. you smell in her underpants, not a rat.

<u>Uh-Oh 9</u>: Your 26-month-old future gentleman is having a fun afternoon jumping on the couch when your wife walks in and says, "Say, Jack, is this what you call productive time?" You put down your magazine, and smile. "You're right, dearest. I should be setting a better example." At this juncture, you should take a moment to instruct Jack Jr. on proper jumping

technique, then join him.

True or False?

Answer: *True*. Your wife will be horrified and think about every moment she's put you in charge of Jack, the two of you alone, over the past three months. She will instantly (and permanently) reduce the length of her shopping trips by 64%.

Uh-Oh 10: You round the corner and spy your 18-month-old daughter crouched over the coffee table happily licking her just-completed finger painting like it's an ice cream cone. Your first (and proper) reaction is to snatch the painting away and call 911.

True or False?

Answer: *True*. But like so many things in life, your first reaction is, unfortunately, over-reaction. Instead, since you've been intelligent enough to insist on non-toxic paints ahead of time, you should compliment her work by tasting it yourself, remarking on how much you've always wanted a turquoise tongue.

Good job! How you scored doesn't really matter, but you might want to glance at the following chart to see how rank you are...no, I mean how you rank compared to your peers. Total your correct responses and find your corresponding status as a toddler-disaster expert.

OFFICIAL P.U.T./D.A.T. RATINGS

Score	Official Rating
10	SUPERMAN
9	Master of Disaster
8	S.W.A.T. Team Lieutenant
7	Civil Defense Coordinator
6	Bomb Squad Supervisor
5	E.R. Technician
4	Unemployed Paramedic
3	Ambulance Chaser
2	Lost at Sea
1	Captain of the Titanic
0	CRASH DUMMY

When all's said and done, did your disaster drill play out the way you hoped? Are you riding a wave of popularity as a caped crusader/ S.W.A.T. specialist, or near the bottom of the ocean as a seaweed-eating imbecile with a crushed cranium?

Alas, ask any 9th grader with a typical outlook and he will tell you how you rate on tests is highly over-rated. It's how you score with chicks that really counts. And you've already proved your ability to produce at least one or two fantastic results. They're called children.

So rest easy with your results, and don't worry too much what the female population thinks. The women around you have their own agenda, and if you're lucky and behave like a gentleman, they'll include you once in a while. Now is the time to turn your attention away from your own achievements and toward those of your offspring.

Now is the time to learn

The Art of Being Adaptable.

The Art of Being Adaptable

The first thing you need to adapt is your rampaging, crisis-tripping, post-infant's living quarters. Now that your little cherub is a roaming, rambling, ransacking little demon, you need to make toddler-proofing your home the highest priority. Your wife may be ahead of you on this topic, but you do want her to think of you as a handy man, don't you? (Even if you have two left thumbs like I do, at least your heart can be in the right place.)

So your job is to double-check that your home is being adapted to proper toddler-safe specifications. When you're alone in charge, every toddler-proofing addition will give you extra peace of mind. Work with your wife on this. Otherwise, you won't have peace of mind, but instead, a piece of her mind. And that's just not the kind of piece you need, is it?

Consult with an expert (in addition to your wife) if you like. There are professional toddler-proofing businesses in every big town. Lord knows, they're out there ready to take your money like everyone else. Or just use your common sense and look at every component of your home from a toddler's point of view...that is, take a low-down, dirty look at every possible danger.

Finally, check the father-tailored tips in Chapter 2. They will help put you on the right track. Just take care not to fall into a safety-nut rut. Taking safety too far has the potential to send you and your spouse to the loony bin—and no toddler needs a drooling, incoherent parent when it's time for a soothing bedtime fairy tale.

Particularly in the beginning of toddlerhood, you need to be flexible and adaptive to the whirl of changes around you. If Mommy is working and schedules socially-enriching "Playdates" for you and your toddler to attend, be prepared to get spit on, bitten, bopped in the head and pinched on the leg. And that's just what you can expect from the other mothers at the party. The toddlers will probably ignore you.

Seriously, early toddlerhood is a time when you need to stay with the program, go with the flow and sit quietly on your seat in the stern, because male and female, we're all in the same boat. Your wonderchild will continue to make waves of typhoon-like design, and your duty is to hang tight, be resourceful and most of all, don't suck in too much bilge water and drown. Don't forget, in the family, you're sometimes remembered as Captain of the Ship. It may feel like a leaky, tired canoe going upstream, but you still have some say in charting the family's course.

Remember to adapt and try to steer the tribe in the right direction. If you're having trouble adjusting to the current trend, take a look at the following *Toddlerdom Tips for Hip, Happy Pappys*. You never know. Some blustery toddler-care afternoon when your canoe's blown backwards, the oars are ripped from your grip, and you feel on the verge of capsizing...these sensible concepts might help keep you afloat. Otherwise you could find yourself suddenly, you guessed it—up the creek without a paddle.

Toddlerdom Tips for Hip, Happy Pappys

A few random, yet heartfelt suggestions to help you adapt and prepare for a happy post-infantile homelife:

DO stop by your favorite nutrition (or drug) store and stock up on multi-vitamins and Geritol for you and your wife to help give you extra energy to cope with your toddler's nuclear-powered spunk.

DON'T personally think about taking steroids or Viagra because you might start feeling too froggy and pumped up and that's what got you in all this toddler trouble originally, two or three years ago, if you recall.

DO purchase your own (man-size) apron made of stain-resistant fabric with nice, ruffled trim to protect your clothing and make your offspring feel secure during the slop-fests known as toddler mealtimes.

DON'T walk around shirtless near Toddette's high-chair or booster seat because first, she might think you're hairy and scary, then second, you might end up looking like Austin Powers with a chest-full of sghettie-O's.

DO furnish your toddler's playroom with stacks of coloring books, fingerpaints, blocks, pull-toys and reading books to help him stay occupied while you read your favorite magazine in the corner.

DON'T try to get away with strapping your child in a playpen while you watch ESPN's *Sport Reporters* on Sunday morning when your wife's away on business. The same rule applies to any *SportsCenter* segment.

DO project confidence about your toddler-care abilities no matter how vulnerable you feel when Mommy's out of town.

DON'T call your mother-in-law and ask her to explain how this 'toddler-thing' works unless you're ready for her to hop on a plane and pay you another 'extended visit' like the one you enjoyed year before last. Remember?

DO be a strong father-figure and clean up every type of puke, poop, up-chuck, spit-up, snot-plug, hawker, booger-slime and half-eaten food slop with a great, big smile on your face. (But use a towelette, not your face.)

DON'T whine like a baby and throw up yourself when you walk into the dining room and see fecal matter smeared along the baseboard and a three-pound Huggies hanging from the chandelier.

DO stay paternally calm when you're alone and in-charge of toddler activities, keeping reference materials (like this) handy for emergency consultation.

DON'T invite over male or female friends (and especially) relatives because you think there's strength in numbers. Though your guests, no matter how you perform, these people will view you as a weak link in the parental chain, and each will anoint you with barrels of know-it-all toddler-care advice you don't really need.

DO tell your wife how much you love her, as often as you think of it, not only because she will love to hear it, but your toddler will have a good feeling when she hears it, too.

DON'T tell your toddler's infant brother how much you love him (at least not in front of your toddler), because that will stimulate jealousy and unnecessary sibling rivalry, and your toddler might bop both you and her brother over the head with a Duplo as soon as she gets a chance.

DO keep toddlerhood in perspective at all times, and know this time shall pass, and also know the word "No!" will be used no less than 342 times a day until the age of four.

DON'T show up for your father-care session dragging belts, paddles, whips, bolo bats and croquet mallets along to enforce discipline. Your toddler knows physical punishment is obsolete and will only laugh at you.

DO take a nap whenever your toddler takes one, because you need the rest, and also because you can dream about being a tough-guy with a nickname like *The Terminator*.

DON'T mention your dreams to anyone.

DO think about a post-toddler life where you regain your sanity and self-respect, wear regular clothes, have intelligent conversation with other adults, and last but not least, go potty whenever you feel like it.

⌙　　⌙　　⌙　　⌙　　⌙

Chapter two

The Name of the Game Is "Pack Man"

These are <u>really</u> the times that try men's souls
—Thomas Paine
(commenting on his extended trip to Europe with
twin toddlers, following the American Revolution)

Boy, you're gonna carry that weight,
carry that weight, a long time
—The Beatles
(from the famous Abbey Road medley...enlightening tunes about
toddler parenting if you listen to the lyrics closely)

Have you noticed? Post-children, family travel just isn't the carefree experience it once was. In the days before fatherhood changed your life forever, you and your lovely spouse could travel light and impulsively any time the mood struck.

Remember when you used to spy a movie or concert in the paper and say, on the spur of the moment, "Hey, Honey. Let's go see so-and-so tonight. It'll be fun!" Recall the romantic weekend jaunts to places like Napa Valley, the Berkshires and the French Quarter?

Now, for the longest time, you and your wife have carried the burden of responsibility that comes with creating little humans in your own image. You look at them and love them. Sometimes, you see yourself. Other times you see the monster from the black lagoon. Or Linda Blair, bed-spinning, in a frightening scene from *The Exorcist*. Or Hannibal Lecter, buckled up and feasting in his high chair.

However you look at her or him, she or he is your abiding obligation now, and whatever your plans are tonight or tomorrow, your toddler's needs are camped out in the front row. In other words, whatever stupendous outing you may have had in mind—you don't just pick up and go. Not now.

The carefree past has passed. Toddlerhood is the present tense. That means whenever you choose to leave your home for more than two minutes, you create a tense situation. You have to plan. Strategize. Put together a list. Or two or three.

Now you know why only single people, childless couples and empty nesters have sports cars.

For you personally, the e-male side of the parenting equation, the hairy parent to your heir apparent, heavy burdens of responsibility are just the beginning of what you will have to carry. Perhaps your rigorous training during infant transportation has already taught you. Whenever you move from point A to B, your wife and offspring will expect you to carry that load, dude.

[34]

Whether you like it or not—and often you won't—you're the official Pack Man, mister. Guess you better start flexing your muscles. 'Cause when it comes to sorting, stacking, hoisting and stuffing...YOU ARE THE MAN, brother. That's the good news.

The bad? Your tour of duty as the *pack-meister* will run approximately 12 to 16 years, give or take. That means, through hernias, slipped discs, ruptured knee joints and busted bladders, you compadré, are stuck in this deal for the *LONG HAUL*. So slap on an Ace bandage, tighten up your truss and step up to the packing plate.

Don't Go Crazy, Brother— Just Go

First off, I think you can afford to keep your cool. After all, nobody's going anywhere until you get all the dadgum stuff assembled, loaded and secured. Obviously you start with a list. Make one for car travel and leave it under a magnet on the refrigerator. This should be the only list you'll need for the next two years or so. You can keep adding to it as you keep adding new vehicles to your driveway.

Here's a common sequence of auto-bloat created by essential toddler-packing needs. You start out modest, frugal, sensible and neat. You keep adding to the list on the fridge. You end up gluttonous, debt-ridden, spaced-out and gargantuan:

Dad's Driveway
Haul of Fame

(In ascending order, based on your perceived packing needs and a change of vehicles every ten months for your child's first 8.33 years)

1. Mini Cooper

2. Volkswagen New Beetle

3. Ford Focus Wagon

4. Toyota Camry

5. Buick Roadmaster

6. Chevy Tahoe

7. Suburban

8. Hummer

9. Winnebago

10. Greyhound

So what kind of stuff should you strap in your bus? Your wife will leave that mostly up to you. You get to choose. You get to pack. You get to lift. You get to stow. Only if you forget anything—it's your fault. You get the blame. And, you get to hear about it all the way back on the return trip.

That's why you keep adding to the list and trading up from subcompact to recreational vehicle to tour bus.

One Thing Leads to Another...
Pop's Toddler-Targeted
Pre-Departure Packing List

Every family is different. So I'm not going to sit here and tell you what to take. And even though Mommy will certainly have a suggestion or two, for the most part, she will leave it to you. Just the same, you're welcome to take a peek at the classic suggestions below. But don't stop there. Get going and add your own junk.

'Cause trust me, you won't feel like a true 21st century toddler-*macher* until you're over-burdened and buried in piles of superfluous "essentials." This list, designed with two-year-olds in mind, is merely a token prelude to where you're headed.

You go, boy.

Port-a-Crib or Rollaway Bed

Bed Rail for rollaway

Overpriced, cutsey-pootsey designer Bed Linens

Oversized Playpen or Complete Indoor Playground

Portable air conditioner

Portable humidifier

Barrel of Toys

Wagon (Little Red)

Wagon (Conestoga)

Shelf of Toddler Picture Books

Shelf of Parenting Reference Books

Audio monitor

Video monitor

High Chair or Dining Chair Booster

Ice Chest of Toddler finger foods

Open Bucket of Toddler Travel snack foods

Toddler Backpack

Toddler Trail Mix

Automobile window shades

Tour bus blackout curtains

Car Seat or Toddler Auto Booster Seat

Blankie (favorite)

Blankie (spare)

Regular umbrella stroller

Reclining cycle stroller

Jogging stroller

Diaper bag (if your wife forgets this, you're a dead man)

Extra diapers and/or training pants

Vomit bag (for you, not for your toddler)

Portable potty (indoors)

Port-a-John (outdoors)

Earplugs (in-ear)

Earplugs (spare)

It must be stressed—and believe me, there's a lot of stress related to toddler travel—that the above items are designed for automobile (or semi-truck) travel on interstate, turnpike or autobahn. We're talking about overland travel that features *rubber tires touching asphalt.*

Toddlers just aren't made for any type of transportation where the rubber tires leave the asphalt. Put another way, if the craft you're riding in needs wings or rudders to maneuver, you'd better hope no toddlers are aboard. Even the sweetest moms on the planet generally agree. Air travel and toddlers just don't mix. That's why you only need one list on the fridge.

If you care to experience your own personal flight of terror, just book one short, one-way journey by jet with a toddler under your wing. Thereafter you'll be more than ready to take it slow and steady, one milepost at a time. Only pausing occasionally, dreamlike, to smile, glance in the rear view mirror and adjust your earplugs.

First Wait,
Then Weight

Of course, while you're becoming a beast of burden, hefting all that weight, you must also practice the *Toddler-Wait*. It doesn't matter if you're the CEO of a Fortune 500 company. You could be a senator. County commissioner. President of your homeowner's association. Nobody cares how packed your PDA is with urgent appointments, e-mails and corporate agendas. Your laptop could be burning a hole in its travel case, ready to go to work. It doesn't matter.

You're going to be late. You're practicing the *Toddler-Wait*.

If your toddler's along for the ride, you're going to be late whether you're going to Cousin Jane's or the gym. Bound for the beach on a carefree holiday? Set your mental clock forward an hour or two. Your schedule comes second. Cue up Todd's needs first and foremost.

You got up before dawn and got the wagon packed in record time? You remembered the portable potty and the puke bag and extra pair of earplugs? Good. Relax. Rest your sparkplugs. You're not going anywhere till the traffic heats up proper and you pull onto the street really good and behind schedule.

Prior to departure, that esteemed offspring of yours, the girl-wonder who zips around like a dynamo on wheels, will suddenly become a limping slug with anchors chained to her ankles. Why does your contemporary jet-powered wind-jammer suddenly become the classic *Slowboat to China*?

Could be lots of reasons...

-She doesn't feel like visiting...Aunt Bertha and Uncle Herman bore her

-She hates her car seat

-She simply loves to annoy you and her mother

-She's tired of sitting in the back of the bus

-She's just plain tired

-She has to go potty (again)

-She's hungry

-She's hungry for attention

-You left her blankie at Aunt Bertha's last time

-Aunt Bertha returned the blankie, but washed it beforehand—big mistake

-It's raining and she's afraid to get wet

-It's sunny and it hurts her eyes

-She and her Panda are having a tea party—you're not invited

-It's naptime, she could—but won't—sleep in the car

-It's time for her 10 o'clock tantrum—maybe later

⌐   ⌐   ⌐   ⌐   ⌐

Childproofing Tips—
Making Your Home Safe
for the Next Catastrophe

One thing's for sure. Toddler care is full of contradictions. Hurtling into infinity, a blur before your eyes, your irresistible toddler herself is a wild and wonderful, elusive contradiction in action. Yet there's another paradox you may not have plugged into your busy travel schedule.

The truth is, generally speaking, it's more dangerous to stay home than it is to travel.

As an informed father-figure, you're doubtless aware that statistics show more accidents happen at home than on the road. Just as more accidents on the road happen close to home. By now these facts should lead you to believe that your home is a magnet for accidents, inside and out. After all, you've been *Keeping the Baby Alive till Your Wife Gets Home* for a while.

You've been through the baby-hazard basics, buying gross quantities of items such as electric outlet covers, rubber cushions for sharp corners, safety latches for cabinets and the like. But toddlers demand new assessments. As you're experiencing toddler growth, you can see first-hand how they're becoming taller, faster, stronger, bolder, cleverer, more adaptable and deadly.

Let's say you and your 2-4T youngun are spending a leisurely, stay-at-home afternoon together. No one is calling

Pack-Man to the rescue. The Winnebago sits quietly in the drive. Your packing list rests on the fridge and your empty luggage relaxes behind closet doors. This is the perfect time to take stock of the homefront and evaluate your toddler-proofing talent.

Detouring Toddler-Disaster— a Few Tips for Unflappable Pops

—If you're packing up for a getaway or packing it in to stay, don't stack items too high (for little climbers) and don't leave latches undone (for pinching little fingers).

—Tie a pair of jingle bells to front and back doors. You'll always know when a little person tries to put the slip on you, plus you'll have one less decorating chore for the holidays.

—Care about your electronic gear? Get it up and out of the way. Don't leave dangling cords that pull down deadly blunt instruments of destruction on top of delicate toddler brain tissues.

—Enjoy replacing your wife's precious collectibles at outrageous prices? Protect them, store them, lock them away. Perhaps they will help pay for a college education after appreciating for 16 years.

—Like a caged tiger, your toddler will try to get past them, but put safety gates at the top and bottom of staircases.

[43]

—Put decals on sliding glass doors at toddler eye-level...help eliminate head-busting glides that stop painfully short of the great outdoors.

—Swallow your pride and stash anything your sonny boy might choke on—if it's lying around and he can fit it into his mouth, it's a candidate for calamity.

—Eliminate access to anything poisonous, not just in bathrooms and kitchens, but how about the carport and shed with your delicious chrome cleaners and tasty fertilizers?

—Got cooking duty? Be sure to adapt both stove an oven to toddler-proof status. Otherwise, you'll get burned on your next mommy-administered/toddler-duty assessment.

—Forget all of the above and, for five to six years, seal the inside of your house, lawn and garden in acres of bubble-wrap packing material. If you, your wife and daughter find this inconvenient, hire a pair of ex-Secret Service agents as live-in nanny/*body* guards.

Chapter three

The Toddler Table: Serving Whine with Every Meal

⅃   ⅃   ⅃   ⅃   ⅃   ⅃   ⅃

Give them great meals of beef and iron and steel,
they will eat like wolves and fight like devils
—Shakespeare

No question, you and your wife have been worried about your toddler's diet since day one. During her baby days, you were justifiably distressed about what she ate. First, breast milk, then breast milk and formula, then fruit juice and cereal slop, then strained vegetables, then jars of baby food solids, and finally, real table food.

Now that your Toddlerette sits on a booster seat at the table with you, the focus has shifted. Yes, you're still concerned about what she eats—but it's often what she won't eat that gives you fits.

Especially when the two of you are alone, you ask yourself lots of questions. With horrific table manners and a rotten attitude toward healthy offerings, your toddler (male or female) is a riddle wrapped in a fajita, rolled up in play dough. His/her mental menu is one big fat mystery and like an uncomfortable customer in a snobbish gourmet restaurant with French calligraphy on parchment, you have no idea what he or she might serve up next. And as second-shift Commander of the Kitchen, you're unsure what to serve him or her.

But you know the dining experience at either end— stove to table—will somehow end up frying your nervous system. So you make a decision.

Now, rather than worry yourself silly with what your progeny's food intake will be next, you search for explanations regarding his or her barbaric behavior. In other words, you're going beyond what your toddler's eating, you're trying to figure out...

What's Eating
Your Toddler

Don't let your darling toddler pull your food chain. As long as you're happy with Mommy's suggested menu, don your apron, put the cutting board in position and start feeling right at home on the range. You've got things covered, pots and pans included. As the clan's Ruling Pater, you're now an old-hand at slicing a carrot and smashing a tater.

But still, you keep wondering...why does your toddlerette only like bad foods and rarely the good? Why does she play with her food and dump it on the floor when you're not looking? Why does she say "NO!" to everything healthy and "ME WANT!" to everything sugary and bad? When you take her out to a kid-friendly restaurant for breakfast every four months or so, why does she ignore her favorite french toast, and instead, start kicking the underside of the table so hard the plates look like they're dancing?

What's eating your toddler, anyway?

Well, if you're like me, you're just an everyday dad, not an expert on nutrition, culinary technique or preschool psychology. But. as fellow fathers, I think we can make a few common sense observations.

It seems to me that when it comes to food and eating habits, we parents tend to bring a lot of baggage with us to the toddler table. We were all raised a certain way in our family dining rooms and we all have definite likes and dislikes in food. Suddenly, when our babies turn into toddlers, we see them as little people. Little people who should eat like we do and think like we do at the table.

Worst of all, these little people sense from the get-go that we're determined to make every bite a really BIG DEAL. Whether it's a ban on sweets, a bribe involving treats, bouts over broccoli or nagging over nuggets, every toddler knows we're having a cow when it comes to eating. And we've got lots of beefs about meals and manners.

Consequently, whenever we park him tableside, he expects us to be in his face before the cheese pizza has a chance to get there.

Maybe, just maybe, it might be a worthwhile quest to lighten up a little and explore a less tension-filled approach. Offer a mom-prescribed healthy-choice menu—but have a comfort-food back-up plan in case you need one. Let your tod-dette eat the same thing two or three meals in a row if it's good food she likes. Serve up carrots and beans, but grab a grater and sprinkle cheese on top.

Yet, the truth is, there are no easy answers when you're talking about the riddles of the toddler table. Through the cen-turies, it's too bad our forefathers didn't spend more time tak-ing care of their children. If so, perhaps we modern men would have the wisdom and lore that would lead us to greater toddler enlightenment.

But don't give up hope. Even a humorous book like this has a few father-focused answers (though none too serious). Perhaps a lighthearted test with crazy, mixed-up questions and answers will inspire you toward an enlightened, lightened up method of toddler food management.

If Mommy's away and the stove's ablaze...if the dining room spew is a gooey maze...when the booster seat quakes and the chair leg breaks...after you slip on the splatter-mat and fall on your face...that's when you need a serious sense of humor about your topple from grace. And while you're testing your sense of humor, a revelation or two about the mysteries of toddler-eating (er, feeding, I should say) won't do you any harm.

So sink your teeth into a challenge that gets straight to the meat of the problem. What's the point in sugar-coating it? Every feeding frenzy contains multiple opportunities for disaster. That's why we cooked up a multiple choice examination of your toddler-keyed intestinal fortitude.

Speaking of toddlers, you'll note that *Dad's Bad Day at the Toddler Cafe* is an oral exam. That means you can read it out loud if you like. Just don't read the answers out loud before you read the questions. That would be cheating, and cheaters get no dessert.

Saddle up to the chuck wagon and take your chances, pardner. Then look for your official culinary degree at the conclusion of the test.

⌐   ⌐   ⌐   ⌐   ⌐

DAD's BAD DAY
AT THE TODDLER CAFE
Oral Exam

Question:

Instead of sharing with his four-year-old sister when asked, your 28-month son tries to shove a chocolate chip cookie in her ear. Should you?

(a) Reserve a spot for him in medical school...ear, nose and throat specialty
(b) Ask your daughter if she'd like an in-ear Oreo instead
(c) Tell him sternly, "That's a crumby thing to do," then crumble the cookie over his head and say, "See what I mean?"
(d) Ignore the incident completely

The answer is
Naturally, (d). In the daily tug of war known as sibling rivalry, this is your basic non-event. Make a big deal out of it and you're certain to see more of the very same action. With (a), you narrow his choice just a tad early. I mean, who knows, gynecology might be his thing. You already know your daughter (b) loves Oreos, so why ask? Don't think about (c) unless you enjoy the extra time and labor involved in washing his hair for the third time in eight hours.

[50]

Question:

Your wife leaves instructions for you to feed your sweet two-year-old toddlerette specially prepared squares of buttered toast. You serve up a generous portion. After going to the bathroom, you return to find Kitty on the table, hunched over the plate, sharing the treat. Should you?

(a) Whack the cat over the head with a broom
(b) Tell your daughter she should include you the next time she puts together a guest list
(c) Tell the cat his big brother the St. Bernard is looking for him
(d) Invite your St. Bernard in to enjoy breakfast with the three of you, then quickly demonstrate for your little girl the concept of family sharing. (CAUTION: If the dog growls, you'd best let him have the big pieces.)

The answer is

Again, (d). Think of the potential vet bills caused by (a); and if you do this, your wife might have you locked in a cage at The Humane Society. Opposite of (a)'s completely negative outcome, (c) will beget NO reaction at all. Of course the St. Bernard is looking for him. You can be sure the cat knows this. You're left with (b) or (d). The first is a sweet, but feeble request—worse still, it's abstract. Toddlers could care less about abstract politeness. (d) demonstrates a confident, concrete solution that makes everybody happy. Only, you'll have to put a second batch in the toaster before you sit down to share.

Question:

Your toddler daughter hasn't eaten vegetables in two weeks. Suddenly she joins in begging when your beagle sits up for a biscuit. Should you?

      (a) Tell her to "Speak!" then stick a string bean in her mouth
      (b) Simply give her a Milk Bone and say, "Good boy!"
      (c) Get the leash, slip a collar around her neck, then take her for a walk to the market for fresh spinach
      (d) Stare at the side of her head and say, "I'm sorry, but whoever bobbed your ears did a terrible job."

The answer is
(a). This is an action-oriented response and solves the problem fast. A superb father-toddler care decision! On the other hand, (b) doesn't solve the problem, plus it's confusing gender-wise. The solution (c) is way too complicated and might be misinterpreted along the sidewalk. Besides, no more than 2% of the toddler population will eat fresh spinach. (d) Your beagle might get a grin out of this commentary, but it's strictly a dead-end.

Question:

It's lunchtime. You're enjoying a cup of coffee at the table next to your hardy-eating two-and-a-half-year-old. The pleasant mood is shattered when she plops a glob of macaroni & cheese in your cup, splashing hot java on the table and in your face. Should you?

(a) Scream in pain
(b) Blink and smile, knowing the superficial burns on your nose will heal quickly
(c) Paste a blue ribbon on her forehead for Best New Pasta Recipe of the Year
(d) Shout, "Yum Yum!" and gobble up the glob you fished out with your fingers

The answer is
(c). For a tough, father-figure type, (a) is very weak—unacceptable. (b) indicates approval for bad behavior, no good. (c) is a wonderfully positive reaction which could lead your daughter into a lucrative culinary arts career. (d) is fine too, setting an excellent example on how to enjoy finger foods, but (c) is more creative and progressive in the long run.

Question:

Against your will, you react to your son's spraying half-masticated green peas on you by upturning a bowl of Jello on his head. At that moment, your wife walks in. Should you?

(a) Say, "Jimmy! What a funny new hat you have!"
(b) Grab the bowl, put it on your head, then make a clown face at your spouse
(c) Slobber at her feet and beg for forgiveness
(d) Spoon up portions of Jello from Jimmy's hair to his mouth, making "Mmmm...mmmm" sounds

The answer is

(b). You can't fool your wife with (a), forget about it. (c)? Where's your pride, for heaven's sake. (d)? Uh, not quite. She'll give you the same response as (a). Admittedly, (b) is an imperfect choice in an embarrassing moment, but it might get a quick laugh and lessen your punishment, at least a tiny notch or two.

Question:

Your beautiful Trish won't eat her sauteed carrots for the fourth straight weekend. Should you?

(a) Grab a pair of antique rabbit ears from the basement TV, then perform a bizarre impression of Bugs Bunny to take her mind off how bad they taste
(b) Let the hamster loose on Trish's plate
(c) Tell Trish you hate carrots too, then dump them in the disposal
(d) Buzz her high-chair with a carrot-filled spoon, calling "Open the hangar, Carrot Concorde's landing!"

The answer is

(c). You might poke yourself or Trish in the eye with (a), too risky and ironic when it comes to carrots. Avoid (b). Who needs greasy, orange-colored rodents running around? Your daughter knows (d) is a toddler-feeding cliché if she ever heard one—too crude for her sophisticated taste. Ah, (c)! Sweet revenge for all the times your mother tried to make you eat rabbit food.

Question:

At breakfast, Grand Uncle Harry dines across from you and your 34-month-old son, complaining ad nauseum about the boy's table manners. Should you?

   (a) Politely request that Uncle lay off the criticism or you're going to give him all-day potty duty
   (b) Smile when Harry ignores you for the third time, then give him a good, swift kick in the shins under the table
   (c) When Harry gasps in pain say, "Little Buster's got a helluva kick for a 3-year-old, doesn't he? Think he should play soccer?"
   (d) When Harry's eyes water and he spits out his food and drops his fork on the floor, innocently comment, "Gee, Unc, your manners aren't so perfect either."

The answer is
You're right, it's <u>all of the above</u>—the most fiendishly unfair of all multiple choice answers, the kind we all hated in school. But you have to admit, it's a beautiful progression from polite request to revenge to cover-up to a point well-made. Better late than never, Uncle Harry needs to learn that toddlers and table manners just don't mix.

Question:

After three years of eating exclusively at home, you risk a night out at a low-key barbecue joint with your toddler. Everything goes smoothly till she rares back and flings a beef rib at the booth across the aisle. The bone bounces off a man's head, taking his toupee with it. Should you?

(a) Scream, "There's a skunk loose in here!"
(b) Compliment Sarah on her lively fastball
(c) Explain to Sarah the difference between a real pitching
     mound and the mound of baked beans on her plate
(d) Tell your waitress you're a health inspector and
     want to know why the ceiling tiles are falling

The answer is
That's right, follow your instincts with (a). You might consider
(b) and (c), because Little League instruction can be very
rewarding for dads, sons and daughters. Only, restrict teaching
to outdoor venues, unless you happen to be at Turner Field, sitting at a table in the Chop House. Unless you have a state-
issued photo I.D., your waitress will see right through (d).

Scoring: Test-takers receive ten points for each correct answer.
Total the score and check your professional rating below.

BAD DAY AT THE TODDLER CAFE *Exam*

Score	Culinary Degree
0	Unemployed Dishwasher
10	Drive-Thru Dropout
20	Busboy-Flunky
30	Microwave Assistant
40	Fast Food Manager
50	Cordon Bleu Graduate
60	Iron Chef
70	Respected Restaurateur
80	*FOOD TV* IDOL

DOWN THE HATCH
AND HAPPY

You're the chef du jour until Mommy's return tomorrow from important corporate conferencing three states away. It's noon on your second 24-hour kitchen shift; the dishwasher and sinks are full of clutter and decaying leftovers.

At least your gentlemanly three-year-old is breaking bread quietly in the breakfast nook, strapped securely in his booster seat. Even better, he seemed to like the idea of ravioli and a tossed salad for lunch. Finally, something different. You cluck with satisfaction and turn to click the dishwasher to start.

Quicker than you can say, "food fight," you hear a bang and a crash from across the room, trailed by an animal-sounding moan. You take it in all at once: the scowl at the table, the Ragú dripping from the blinds, the vinegarette-laced romaine impersonating wallpaper.

"Want teanut dutter!" your son cries. "Not wettuce. *Teanut dutter!*"

Like the cafeteria monitor in the movie *Animal House*, you sigh heavily and stride to the scene of the crime. You think about how your role as lunchroom sergeant-of-arms (and legs and noses and tongues and teeth) makes you feel weary and old. You survey the aftermath of your toddler's aborted "luncheon" and wonder which janitorial service you can call to fire-hose the table before applying germ-killing disinfectants to the area. Hold the phone. Sure enough, the dog and cats have

[57]

heard and smelled snacktime in the making, and they are already hunkered down in full-tilt feast mode.

Wise and adaptable papa, what will you do now?

Simple. You get the Peter Pan and the grape jelly out of the cabinet and you make *teanut dutter & jayrry*. Because you're enlightened and following lightened up toddler-food practices, you can swallow this small defeat and move on.

So what if your son is stuck on peanut butter and you've plied him with it three meals in a row? At least he'll get his fair share of protein, carbohydrates and calcium (from his sippy cup, upturned but now righted). An added bonus is the animals are happy, they've performed a vital cleaning service, and you don't have to feed them this evening, just junior.

Yes, your kitchen is a disastrous mess and the rest of your home is soon to follow, room by room. *The Terror of Toddlerville* is on the loose again and you can't erect barricades fast enough to contain him. You can only stop him long enough to wipe-free excess jelly and tomato sauce creeping into eyes, ears and nose. Did any of the food actually make it into his oral cavity? Is it naptime yet?

Later, look on the bright side. Your little rascal asks to go B.M. Potty (all by himself) just before nappie, producing a magnificent specimen you can both brag to Mommy about tomorrow. Plus you know (A the peanut butter isn't clogging up his insides *too* much and (B you're set for a worry-free afternoon, watching the playoffs, sans poop patrol, not even flinching when he squats behind the door during halftime.

The Toddler Food Pyramid

YOUR TODDLER
DOESN'T KNOW BEANS

True. *Keep it Simple* is the best advice you'll ever hear about toddler meal preparation. However, one culinary complication that will rub your guilt feelings raw is the subject of vegetables, cooked or uncooked.

As the scientific illustration on the preceding page indicates, among food types, veggies occupy a lowly spot on the toddler pyramid of choice. As the strong, silent side of the parenting teeter-totter, you might wish to avoid this whole rotten business about vegetable intake in your offspring. And when you first encounter the barbed wire food defense your toddler constructs, "surrender" just might be your first response.

But don't be a cowardly desserter, running to the safety of the refrigerator, passing out chocolate pudding while you leave the cauliflower undefended, rotting in the sink.

You're too brave to keep the broccoli away from the frontline struggle. Mommy is counting on you. Especially when she knows, like Fort Sumter, the Toddler-Veggie Campaign is merely the first battle in a lifelong civil war with your lad or lass.

Alas, this battlefront is a grim landscape of derelict lettuce, torn broccoli spears, battered peas, snubbed rutabaga, and wounded yams. As a toddler-care veteran, all I can say is keep fighting the good fight with veggies as a major objective.

You'll see your toddler change allegiance day-to-day, embracing beans and corn one, then turning traitor the next. In the veggie wars, Toddlers are notorious for switching sides daily.

You might hit a lucky streak, nailing the toddler-target eight days in a row with braised zucchini. And that might be the last time he touches it till kindergarten.

So stay loose, stay light. But when Mommy comes inspecting, remember how to stand at attention in your dress (apron) uniform. And don't forget to pass the peas along with the other food-group ammunition.

⌐　　⌐　　⌐　　⌐　　⌐

Chapter four

Temper Tantrum: The Toddler National Anthem

Oh say, can you see...
through the perilous fight,
O'er the ramparts we watch'd...
the temper's red glare, the bombs bursting in air,
Gave proof thro' the night...
our toddler's tantrum was still there

—With profound apologies
to Francis Scott Key

In *Keeping the Baby Alive till Your Wife Gets Home*, we reintroduced to 21st century dads an earlier historic figure, one of great import to the field of science (and fatherhood), the great man himself, Sir Isaac Newton. After years of painstaking research, we uncovered the truth that Sir Isaac was much more than a great physicist and astronomer.

In fact Isaac was a romantic male with great stamina, a man who would have laughed in the face of Viagra. He fathered ten offspring which he doted upon when he wasn't busy looking at the stars or making more babies.

Yes, gentlemen, Sir Isaac is an inspiration for us all, a man who spoke softly but carried a very big telescope. And he did it all in the name of science.

His brilliant theories on the science of infant feeding went unpublished until recently. Even more recently, unearthed in an old attic in England, the *Clearing Skies Press* research team discovered Newton's theories of toddler behavior. You are reading the results of this astonishing find now.

In studying these complex theories you can't help but marvel at their basis in pure common sense. You can imagine old Isaac in the orchard, peeping around the apple trees, observing his toddlers in action. The result? You guessed it. Newton's famous LAWS OF MOTION.

As fathers of the future world, the only question we might have is, did his toddlers have tantrums nearly 300 years ago?

Throughout the course of time has every barrel always contained a rotten apple? You bet it has. That's exactly why good old Sir Isaac tucked away something amazing for us modern-day dads.

Inside the ancient trunk were NEWTON's LAWS OF THE TODDLER TANTRUM FOR FATHERS, each linked to one of his famous laws of motion...

Newton's First Law of Motion:
a body moving at constant speed
in a straight line will continue unless it is
acted upon by a force

Newton's Tantrum Law Number One:
force will have no effect on a toddler body
in the middle of a tantrum,
so don't bother

. . . .

Newton's Third Law of Motion:
for every action there is a reaction

Newton's Tantrum Law Number Three:
for every reaction to a tantrum
there is increased action of the tantrum,
so don't bother

I can't blame you if you noticed. Unfortunately, Newton's Tantrum Law Number Two is a missing artifact. But, hey, as my dad always told me, two out of three ain't bad. A tip I've found goes a long way with Artifacts, Baseball and Blackjack.

The Sum of All Tantrums

As a hip, happy pappy, what you need to keep in mind is that the sum of all tantrums is not as bad as its parts might indicate. Body parts included. So when you're standing there witnessing your toddler's screaming lungs, flapping arms, twitching legs and heaving torso, keep telling yourself "this *has* to be the worst part of parenting, this *must certainly be* the worst part of parenting..."

But never ask yourself, "What could be worse than this?" Because you're going to find out what's worse in another twelve to thirteen years, whether you think so or not.

In the meantime when the summit of the tantrum approaches, and the intensity and insanity of it are burning your brain like hot lava squirted in your ears—remember— this too shall pass. Don't envy what you don't know...the grass ain't always greener on the other side of the volcano (or playmat). Especially don't envy the quiet toddler strapped in the car parked next to you. That innocent tyke may have just exited the interstate along with a Grade A Fit that had his whiteknuckled mom screeching tires, screaming epithets, and thinking many unhappy thoughts about her toddler.

Repeat morning and night: "All toddlers misbehave. All toddlers have tantrums. My beautiful, intelligent, normal child is no exception."

Besides, to try and stop this type of activity, you might as well step in the ring with a couple of bloodthirsty sumo wrestlers. Even when you see only one body in the ring, your toddler is fighting with himself for control of his body *and* his emotions.

Get in there close and you might get hurt. Like the time your grandmother told you about when she stuck her hand in the washing-machine wringer. (Only if your little one might really hurt himself should you intervene.)

From a paternal point of reference, I know how bad it seems in the middle of a tantrum, when you're on-watch and (supposedly) in control. But this whole phase will fade in both of your memories, part by part, scene by scene, tantrum by tantrum.

Speaking of the intensity of tantrums and their hot lava-flow effect on your brainwaves...as the mature adult on tantrum duty, you need to stay clear-headed and quick-thinking at all times.

Therefore, know clearly that no amount of pleading— even if you do it slithering on your belly like a scheming lizard— will alter a toddler's behavior. You can clasp your hands in a praying formation and cry "please" 300 times. No heart-wrenching "please" or "pleas"of any type will dent the toddler tantrum barrier. No verbal messages will hit their mark.

[67]

You could mount the summit of the tantrum as the newly crowned Oracle of Truth, granted the eloquence of P. T. Barnum and Abraham Lincoln combined. Your spiel could be smoother than your former baby's cheeks. It just won't matter once your toddler blows his top.

You may as well let the tantrum flow. Yelling won't help either, so as Newton advised us, *don't bother*. Besides, when your ticked-off tantrum-head gets his full, furious groove on, the openings to his eardrums clang shut like steel doors in a sinking submarine. At this point the ear canal is flooded and the usual pathway to your child's brain is hermetically sealed.

Just remember. If you're taking care of Toddy-O eight weekends in a row and the uncontrollable fits multiply and mount in your mind, you have to summon your strength, zip your lip, and believe the tantrum sum simply isn't as mountainous as it seems.

You can't let your composure collapse in an avalanche of self-pity, gaping skyward in the center of the supermarket aisle, first blubbering, then bawling out stuff like,

Softly, *"Why me?"* *or worse...*
"For crying out loud!" *or worse...*
"STOP!—in the name of all that's sacred." *or worse...*
"Somebody take over—I can't cope!" *or worse...*
"Adoption Auction—Aisle 3!" *or worst of all...*
Sobbing, *"I WANT MOMMY!"*

[68]

Tantrum Trouble—Dead Ahead

You might well ask, is there any Daddy-Defense at all against the random toddler tantrum? Well, as the saying goes, the best defense is sometimes a good offense. But in this case, offense has more to do with planning than on-the-field action. In your toddler playbook, there is no blocking and tackling allowed. But you can chalk up a good game plan based on smooth classroom-like, blackboard preparation.

The key is anticipation.

You need to calculate, what precisely is lighting the short fuse of your volcanic little sweetheart. What's making his blood boil and her temper erupt?

In your mind, if you can track the trail of tantrums, you might be able to see one coming and squeeze right by it.

Do they start most often when she's tired or hungry?
-Dropped off for daycare/left with a sitter?
-After you come home from work?
-At the grocery store (*a classic tantrum site*)?
-In the quiet of the library (*yikes!*)?
-Visiting friends or relatives?

Is the tantrum hitched to a recurring theme?
-Mealtime arguments?
-Snacktime disagreements?
-Toys, to share, not share, abuse, or lose?
-Television, turned on, turned off, tuned in, tuned out?
-Naptime, bathtime, bedtime or worse yet, Mommy-
Daddy quiet time?

[69]

If you can pinpoint the time and place of the average ugly outburst, perhaps, as Big Chief in Charge, you can exert a speck of paternal control and head the vile behavior off at the pass. Wouldn't that be a beautiful thing?

Distraction is a tried-and-true ploy that still works with toddlers (sporadically) like it did back in their infant heyday. This is where common sense puts your sense of humor on a pedestal, stage-light gleaming :

Make a Face   Dance a Jig

Make a Joke   Act the Fool

Be a Nerd   Slap Your Knee

Hum a Tune   Imitate Opera Man

Pretend You're a Chipmunk, Piglet, Donkey, Penguin

Whistle like a Loon   Hop like a Bunny

Make Foghorn Noises   Chug like a Choo-Choo

Do Play-by-Play Commentary like You're the
Master of Ceremonies at a State Fair Freak Show

⌐   ⌐   ⌐   ⌐   ⌐

Tantrum Researchers...Dedicated, Tireless

Begging for Trouble with Rewards and Ransoms

One of the biggest temptations of father-toddler care is to surrender to the awesome power of the tantrum. Sure, the fury of it is a scary sight. Not just for you, but for your toddler, too. Can you imagine? It must be like being in the vortex of a tornado, looking at a world turned upside-down and inside-out.

But that's just about enough sympathy on this subject. We parents are the ones who deserve a little of that. And that's about how much sympathy our toddlers will give us. Very little.

What you must know, as Daddy Long-Legs, is that you're expected to stand tall in the tantrum department. That means you can't give up and throw in the towel like a used-up pugilist with rubber legs and cauliflower ears. Most of all, you can't yield to the temptation of begging and bribes.

Write this reminder on a notecard and slip it in your apron pocket:

Dads Don't Beg—Dogs Do

You can't start waving candy bars and ice cream treats in front of a toddler's face before, during or after a stormy episode. Your little cyclone with the pudgy knees and plump bellybutton might slow the action for half a second, giving your payola a lightning-quick look. But it's going to take a lot more than a nutty-butty cone to wind down this tornado.

And what would your cowardly act accomplish if it really worked?

Are you and your neighbors ready for a full-blown flip-out on the pavement opposite your doorstep every time the ice cream truck yodels by?

Ransom is for slimeball kidnappers and gutless dictators, not crusading toddler-pops. Appeasing unacceptable, barbaric behavior didn't work against the Nazis, and it's not going to work now. Once you start giving in, it's tough to set a limit on what you have to give.

Indeed, you will need (but not deserve) a ton of sympathy if you let your toddlerette start using her tantrums as a tool. If she thinks she can get her way by stomping, shaking and twitching...if she learns the art of color-switching, say from blood-vessel-popping red to breath-held-fainting blue... then papa, your terrible Twos are about to take a turn for the worse.

Here's the ticket. On the toddler journey to pre-school country, there are potholes, bumps and detours aplenty. *NOT* letting her have her way via tantrum will help you pave the way for a happier daddy-todd direction. When, you ask?

Somewhere down the road.

But ransoms and bribes aren't the only sinkholes on the toddler-tantrum highway. Premium tank-fulls of daddy-induced promises and rewards might also talk your careening toddler-mobile into a momentary halt. The problem is, rewarding future good behavior with special prizes is the proverbial road to ruin.

Let's say it's Sunday afternoon and you and your 35-month-old buckaroo are taking a relaxing stroll in a restful, oak-lined park. Suddenly your mild-mannered young man gets caught up in the questionable idea of catching a squirrel.

Your son goes temporarily insane.

Following the rodent, he tries to vault a bench and tumbles to the turf. This action trips his tantrum switch, and seeing those familiar tremors begin, you leap to the rescue. As he shakes his fists and foams at the mouth, you slip up behind and grasp him firmly under the shoulders.

Now's when you should keep your calm and tell sonny that furry squirrelies might look cute, but they have sharp little teeth designed to bite. You could pick up an acorn and crunch it between your molars as an example.

Sadly, instead of informing him authoritatively that wild creatures often carry rabies, or even the Bubonic plague, many fathers would decide to unload a bushel-basket full of dubious pleasures and promises.

If you happened to be an innocent bystander enjoying the nature and fresh air of a parkland outing, it wouldn't be very rewarding to listen to a stream of worm-grubbing rewards such as:

Be Good and you can have a hot fudge sundae for supper.

Be Good and I'll buy you a really expensive toy.

Be Good and it's McDonald's Happy Meals morning, noon and night.

Be Good and Sunday before lunch we'll watch *Little Toot* together 16 times instead of the final round of the British Open.

Be Good and you can poop in your pants all week.

Be Good and you're going to Disney World twice-a-year for the rest of your life.

What could have been a great demonstration of woodlands know-how and park-ranger-like expertise becomes a wimpy trail of sugary promises, groveling guarantees, lowly kowtows, and slavish assurances.

Basically, you'd be telling your three-year-old that the world will lie at his feet and kiss his toes anytime he chooses to act like a normal human for a few minutes. That message is just a tad misleading. He might grow up expecting a big bag of goodies for *Not* making an "F" or *Not* burning the house down or *Not* stealing your keys and taking your Austin-Healey for a spin in the lake.

At that rate, before very long, you'd be running out of patience, cash and insurance, as well as rewards.

Better to tough it out with a basic, no-frills cool-daddy-attitude toward boiling-hot tantrum behavior. Something like, "Okay, little buddy. If you're determined to have a fit, I'm determined to stand right beside you and wait it out.

"When you calm down, we can talk about how you feel, if you feel like it. You can tell me what made you so upset. Words are good. But let's talk in calm words. Yelling is no good. Hitting isn't good. For you or me."

And if serene, modern reasoning doesn't summon a little daddy-magic, we can, once again, turn to our forefathers. Even before Newton's time, the toddler-disorder was examined and faithfully documented by ancient toddler-historians.

Now, the Clearing Skies Press archaeological team proudly presents an astonishing discovery, even more ancient and revealing than *Isaac Newton's Laws of the Toddler Tantrum.*

For the first time, before your eyes, absorb one of the most significant artifacts ever created for fathers by our ancient brethren.

Discovered just recently under the voluminous rubble surrounding the ruins of Pompeii, we present—exclusively—for your paternal enlightenment, rare words of wisdom. On an ancient stone tablet, cracked in two but now restored, our Roman forebearers gave us the amazing *Ten Commandments of Toddler Tantrums*, unveiled here in their original form.

Study them, learn them, live them. Our toga-draped patriarchs witnessed the evils and irony of the tantrum, and composed a wise and lucid set of guidelines.

Yea, verily, before the toddler-volcano consumed them, ironically turning legions of tantrum-fighters into vapor, the boys got together in a trusty quorum, thereby making this monumental gift to us.

⌐   ⌐   ⌐   ⌐   ⌐

The Ten Commandments of Toddler Tantrums

1. As mother and father, thou shalt be honored by many tantrums.

2. Thou shalt not kill thy toddler even though thou will feel like it every time thou are honored.

3. Thou shalt not covet your neighbor's toddler who is tantrumless at the moment.

4. Thou shalt not throw thyself in the middle of the tantrum because thy shall suffer the gravest consequences unto thee.

5. Thou shalt bless the times between tantrums and remember them, because these are times to cherish, truly.

6. Thou shalt not bear false witness to thy babysitter about thy toddler's angelic behavior.

7. Thou shalt not steal cookies and chips off thy supermarket shelf using tantrums as a false pretext.

8. Thou shalt not take thy toddler's name in vain, even when thy tongue is

severely tempted, before, during and after a tantrum.

9. Thou shalt not take photographic images of thy toddler's tantrum and place them before frightened relatives.

10. Thou shalt not commit the adultery of asking thy toddler to act like an adult when thy knowest thy toddler is a toddler, and thy also knowest, verily, that adults act like toddlers (and sometimes like babies) on occasion and know the sin of tantrums too.

⌐   ⌐   ⌐   ⌐   ⌐

Chapter five

How Not to be a Weenie When It's Time to Wean

Yet I do fear thy nature;
It is too full of the milk of human kindness

—Shakespeare

⌐   ⌐   ⌐   ⌐   ⌐   ⌐   ⌐

Quick!

Think of three practical reasons why any intelligent little human would want to trade the contents of his or her mother's tender breast for warmed-up broccoli out of a jar.

Time's up.

[81]

Exploring the *Great Milky Way* and a Few of its Mysteries

When you think about it for two seconds, you can't help but believe this is one of Toddlerville's most disheartening assignments. Talk about hard-to-break habits! Getting your toddler to jump off the bottle/breast milk train has to be one of life's more amazing tricks. Why in the world would he or she want to swear off the stuff? It's warm. It's sweet. It's white nectar from the gods—and it's served up from one of God's more incredibly lovely designs, the lovable, lappable, awe-inspiring female nipple.

You remember, don't you?

So how can we unravel this mystery and lend a smidgen of credibility to our role as the he-male caretaker? First, we can monkey around a mile or two in our toddler's shoes. Try to get in touch with your former infant's feelings about weaning, from his head down to his toes. Try to see the situation from his innocent eyes.

Start by accepting a big-picture, cosmic approach to your toddler's feelings about milk, bottles and breasts. As dads, we instinctively realize that these are three pretty fine items. Even if you don't drink milk yourself anymore, it's easy to think back to your childhood days...a warm summer morning when you grabbed the bottle from the fridge and splashed a heaping bowl of frosted flakes with bubbly, fresh milk. Or coming home from a hot, sweaty Little League game and gulping the white stuff cold from the carton. Boy, howdy! Those were the days, huh?

Now think back just a tad further...get in touch with your subconscious and start tapping into images of toddling along with a comforting bottle nippled between your tiny teeth. Think of how it felt to have the ba-ba always by your side, in your grasp, yours whenever you liked. The good white stuff was yours, all yours, even if you left the bottle in some corner for five hours and the cat shared a little. The bottle, the creamy stuff, and the rubbery nipple it squirted from was your thing. Your one and only, main squeeze.

BAM! NO! OUCH! Out of the blue, some well-intentioned, yet ruthless, do-gooding adult marches in and snatches your ba-ba away and hands you a hard plastic sippy cup.

Naturally, you take that little cup by its stupid little handle and fling it across the room into the entertainment armoire. You watch, fascinated as the stupid sippy cup and its idiotic Elmo decal smash into the television screen. The top blows off and the silly little vessel spills its creamy contents across the screen.

Being an intelligent toddler you stutter-step over to the TV, slap the palm of your chubby hand on the glass and smear the milky film around in the form of a Rorshach blot. The faces of The Rugrats, now playing, seem to stare at you from inside the screen, grinning approval.

You think to yourself, "why are they doing this to me? What did I do to deserve this cruel treatment. What's up with this unhappy, unfair, unhealthy nipple-ban?"

It all started, lifetimes ago it seems, when the parental know-it-alls declared Mommy's num-nums as forbidden territory. I LOVED THEM! I LOVED SNUGGLING WITH MOMMY! Suddenly, one day for no reason—with no warning—no more snuggling with Mommy. No more num-nums. Instead, they apologized, and looked away, handing me the fake ba-ba nipple.

"This," the Daddy One said, "is your permanent num-num now. See the nice nipple? You like your formula and I have personally warmed it to the perfect Mommy-like temperature. Try it. You'll see. The ba-ba is now your MAIN SQUEEZE."

"Right," you say to your year-old self. Then you look up at old Pops who is now looking guilty. He sees the question in your eyes.

"For as long as you like," Pop replies. Then in his deep, sincere, daddy-tone. "Go ahead. It's yours."

But you are a human, a little small in human terms, but still human. You don't reach out for the artificial breast like a trained circus dog. No. Instead you choose to torment your father by ignoring him. Your baby face takes on a faraway look and you go back just a bit further in your mind...to when you were a wee bit of a human, weeks-old instead of months. Your lips surround a wet, warm, supple nipple... every human's real and eternal MAIN SQUEEZE.

[84]

You smile and snuggle.

You know in your heart this is the place to be. Now until the end of time you know this to be true and no one can ever convince you otherwise. But they keep trying.

These parents—huge humans, always leaning over with deep voices and bad breath—ply their fraud and trickery. They give you Mommy and make you think she's yours forever. Then they sneakily start substituting a phony rubber breast filled with unknown powder mixed with water. They take Mommy away and the bogus ba-ba takes her place. Permanently.

You grow. In time we all learn to love the ba-ba. Even after some of us hear the whispered truth that the powder the parents mix is not even a milk product. It's more of that vegetable-yuk...akin to the junk force-fed us out of jars. Something called soybean.

But we learn to love the doggone bottle anyway and then, these giant master-humans treat us worse than the average dog. Not even like bright, step-n-fetch-it circus dogs. No sir. They treat us exactly like stray, mangy mutts. These oppressive parental units do us dirty... lowdown, dog-dirty.

Do you know what these towering, lowlife custodians do? They walk up to you one fine day, reach down and take away the ba-ba, too.

Talk about cheats and thieves and lessons learned.

[85]

How in the world does one trust his fellow human if this is truly how the world works? Can you respect family members who lie to young toddlers?

Though an early tragedy of life, the above weaning scenario serves a vital purpose. It teaches each of us to be wary of the world, and to know that the world is full of promises and disappointments.

Most of all, it teaches a kid not to trust every adult who walks up smiling with a gift in his hand. And that's a darn good lesson at any age.

⌙　　⌙　　⌙　　⌙　　⌙

A Subject Close
to Your Wife's Heart

Fortunately for us guilty papas there is a silver lining to this milky cloud called *weaning*. Early on, there is a limit to the decision-making we can make on our own. You can beat your chest and/or spend five hours per day doing pectoral exercises. But the fact of the matter is, the Big Man Upstairs equipped us very poorly for the intimate experience of breastfeeding. At least from the giving end of the business.

Therefore, when it comes to breast-weaning, your wife will surely have more intense feelings—inside and out—on the subject. And choosing the time to wean also lends itself to individual considerations. We needn't go into them here. Just know it is a Mommy-decision and if she feels like sharing her reasoning with you—she will. Otherwise, stick to your own business and wait for the headline-announcement that breast-weaning is underway.

THIS IS GREAT NEWS!

Great because, of all the critical decisions to be made in the melody of your offspring's life, you get to skip a beat with breast-weaning. Let this be music to your ears. Since you happen to be second fiddle in the parenting orchestra pit, you get to take a relaxing snooze during this prelude.

Your darling spouse may leave a note for you here and there. You may be called upon to orchestrate special snacks and drinks to help blunt your progeny's gluttonous appetite for breast milk. For example, at dawn's early light, when your child breaks the calm with the piercing cries of a breast milk addict going through withdrawal, yours could be a solo act for breakfast.

Good luck with the formula, fruit juice and cereal slop. You'll probably do fine...even if you're *not* Mommy and your chest is about as interesting as plywood.

If your child reaches out for your chest, searching for

something soft and round, don't slap her hand and scream something infantile, like, "*NO TOUCH! ME NOT MOMMY!*"

Instead, test the temperature of the formula on your wrist, set a memorable example by making loud slurping/sucking sounds with your mouth, then hand the baba over. You might want to finish up with a loud chorus from the old Campbells soup commercials..."Mmmm...Good! Mmmm...Good! Daddy's boiled milk formula is mmmm...Good!"

At this point, with any luck, your daughter should be confused enough to take the bottle and drain it whether she wants to or not.

Forgive us if we seem to be backtracking here. Chances are, in your neatly organized toddler-household, the topic of breast-weaning is as old as last season's Super Bowl champs. Notice how hard it is to remember, one year to the next, who exactly won the Super Bowl or the Kentucky Derby or the PGA Championship? It's a sign of age, I suppose.

Or perhaps a sign that babies and toddlers slowly take over your brains and you're eventually left with very little space for storing yesterday's sporting events.

Anyway, your toddler abode was most likely done with *breast*-weaning some time ago, and now Pa, you're faced with the painful obligations of *bottle*-weaning.

Unlike breast-weaning, the subject of bottle-weaning remains unclose to anyone's heart.

[88]

Nipping Nipples in the Bud, Bud

Mate, the foremost fact you'll find out about bottle-weaning is that every relative in your family over the age of 23 believes she is the world's foremost expert on the subject.

Take all of their advice with a grain of salt, throw it in a salt shaker and throw it over your shoulder (on the front lawn) for good luck. Then do your own research, listen to your wife and talk about it.

Concentrate on your toddler. Every child is different, yet most pediatricians (or wanna-be pediatrician/friends & relatives) have a timetable in mind for your mini-me. Just remember, your youngster needs his or her own customized timeframe for kicking the bottle habit.

If there's one thing everyone agrees on—impossible, perhaps—it's that putting an infant/toddler down for a nap or nighttime with a bottle in her mouth is bad news, baby. Even a thin film of sour milk resting between cheek and gums through hours of sleep leads to two things:

1) the most terrible toddler breath on the planet
and
2) tooth and gum rot

Now, you can live with the first problem, but your tot certainly can't live with the second. He/she's still getting teeth in—you don't want them to fall out right away, even if they are called "baby" teeth.

But as an enterprising parent, your wife will undoubtedly pass along to you a few tricks of the nipple-busting trade. Not dirty tricks, mind you, but workable tricks just the same. One classic ploy is to trade your todd's ba-ba for a binky at naptime. (Binky is another term for pacifier—one of those "cute" words you're supposed to know, but would probably rather not. "Pacie," short for pacifier, is interchangeably cute.)

I know, as we've talked about before, these too-cute toddler words can make your teeth hurt worse than sour milk. But if you refuse to use them, the Mommies of the world will give you dangerous looks and call you "uppity" behind your back. When your little girl goes "nite-nite," for heaven's sake, she shoves a rag doll in your face and you kiss it on the lips.

Verbalizing "binky" is no big deal, believe me.

Of course, trading binkies for bottles is like offering a wine-o Budweiser for Boones Farm. The crutch, the attachment, the addiction is still in place. And binkies don't do your toddler's mouth any favors, either.

Your spouse has other tricks up her sleeve besides binkies. Newfangled sippy cups with bottle-like looks and nipple-like spouts might work. A comfort object like a blanket or pillow ("blankie" or "lovey" to you, cute-stuff) could replace the binky. Serving only water in bottles but saving the good stuff—such as fruit juice and cow's milk—for the cup might help your todd turn more in a ba-ba-less direction.

Some folks go so far as to splash a drop of bitter lemon or similar liquid on top of the bottle nipple. But your child just might be smart enough to feed *that* to the cat *first* before resuming his sucking routine. In our house, the cats generally suffered enough toddler abuse without that extra bit of torture.

All in all the best course is probably to take it slow and easy for any type of toddler-nipple weaning.

In other words, just because you think it's time to wean, don't throw out every ba-ba in the house along with your (former) baby's bath water. Introduce the sippy cup gradually.

Also, look for signs of readiness. Perhaps, as the alert paternal one, you alone noticed a telltale interest in cups in recent days. But that, ya big mug, doesn't mean you hand your sweet toddlerette a hot cup of java just because you're sitting together at the breakfast table. And even if it's springtime, you don't need to line up 14 cups on the dining room table, each filled with a different color fruit juice like you're dyeing Easter eggs.

No, it means you arrange a special daddy-daughter shopping expedition—a fine springtime tradition, any time of year. But instead of searching for the perfect Easter bonnet, you should let your flirtatious cutie pick out her very own special sippy cup. It doesn't matter if the cup boasts decorations of dragon heads or daffodils as long as it's her choice.

That way when your bottle-loving little lady screams at you for proffering the bedtime mug instead of the precious *bouteille*, what would be the ideal, unruffled, fatherly response?

I'll tell you what. You look over the top of your glasses, hold your finger up for a moment of silence, then whip out your Disney Store sales receipt.

Forceful, focused dads would say, "Who's the quack who selected the Donald Duck cup, anyway?" Then you would remind her that a major part of being an intelligent consumer is making wise purchase decisions. Ending the conversation with, "So drink up, babycakes."

Either that, or you stand up, flap your arms, and make classic cartoon duck noises. Then after your little girl stops giggling, you raise your own cup (carefully hidden behind the table lamp) and say, "Okay, Daisy. Let's toast Donald and his three nephews. You know, don't you, that they *all* drink out of cups like big people. Or, like big ducks, that is."

Preparing for Bottle Battles

Let's say you're lean, mean and ready to help wean. The hero side of your male pride is itching for a challenge. You're thinking, sippy-cup combat, brother. Just drop me right down on the bottle field of battle and I'll capture the hearts of the toddler-enemy with intimidating strength of purpose and silver-tongued diplomacy.

You find yourself daydreaming about it...

As soon as Major Mommy gives me the order, I'll slip around the corner of the sandbox with multiple sippy cups filled with juicy ammunition. The toddler crowd won't know what hit them. They'll surrender to the power of the cup. They'll get no nipples all day and night—and like it. Major Mommy will plan a private award for Private Daddy...a special blue-ribbon, bedroom ceremony for weaning bravery beyond the call of duty.

If those kind of dreams are taking over your brain (and body), then you need a little slap of reality to get you back onto your dull, irritating toddler track. As men, we should know there's no crying in baseball and no glamour in bottle-weaning.

But, Sir Popsalot, if you still think you're ready for a weaning challenge, I think you'll find all the testing you can stand in the upcoming exam. Depending how you score, you might find you're a knight in shining armor, galloping into the sunset toward weaning fame and glory. Or, more commonly, too often, you'll feel like a moat-cleaning, scum-sucking vassal who hasn't a clue about what's going on in his own castle.

One way or the other, you can say our special "Pop" quiz is designed to wean you away from ill-advised thoughts of grandeur about jousting with toddlers and their bottles.

So sharpen your wits and polish your battle shield. Get ready to explore your breadth of knowledge of *The Great Milky Way* and the surreal world of babies, breasts, bottles, bubbles, binkies, and blankies. It's a crazy-quilt, mixed-up time in yours and your toddler's life.

Go ahead, take a gulp. You're on a weaning crusade, so drink it all in. See if you have all the answers he or she needs to kick the habit and come out okay on the other side.

[93]

Sir Popsalot, Crusading Weaner

"Pop" Quiz for Crusading Weenies, Weaners and Winners

Question:

Your half-weaned son discovers Mommy barricaded behind the bedroom chamber door and starts a tantrum, bawling, "Me want milk! Me want milk!" Should you?

> (a) Say loudly, yet calmly, through the door, "Give it up, Ethel. It's back to breastfeeding—there's no way out."
> (b) Place an emergency call to the milk man from your mobile phone
> (c) Sing, "You scream, I scream, we all scream for ice cream."
> (d) Break through the bedroom door with a fire axe

The answer is

(c). The only way you might consider (a) is if you'd like to join the guinea pig in a cage on the back porch. You can't match the equipment, so you can't offer it for use. (b)? Once again, a man isn't your son's first choice. You pick (c) because (d) is yet another bad impression of Jack Nicholson in *The Shining*, and you already did one trying to teach sharing. (c) may not be a solution, but goofball singing can be surprisingly effective in the presence of true tantrum-itis.

Question:

You and 24-month-old Rebecca, successfully weaned, visit her toddler friend next door. Paul, sweet and silent, is five months older but, well, kind of *slow*. Rebecca rattles on, leading him around like a puppy as he sucks on a bottle flopping on his chin. Should you?

> (a) Tell Paul's mom you're sorry her son's retarded and can't kick the habit
> (b) Pluck the bottle from his teeth and say, "Grow up you little punk!"
> (c) Ask Paul's mom if she enjoyed breastfeeding
> (d) Tell Rebecca to play hide-and-seek with Paul while you explain to Paul's mom how *you* feel about breastfeeding

The answer is
(none of the above). Yes, this is a sneaky, nigh-impossible answer, but it serves a worthwhile purpose. That is, to remind each of us how sneaky and impossible to manage our toddlers can be during weaning times. Obviously, in the above scenario, whether you choose (a), (b), (c) or (d), you're headed for trouble. But you already know that if you and Rebecca have been scheduling more than one or two "playdates" a week with Paul and his mom.

Question:

Your 30-month-old toddy-boy guzzles the juice from his sippy cup like a thirsty knight at the Round Table. You figure you have this weaning-thing beat till you discover him crouched in the liquor cabinet guzzling *Crown Royal*. Should you?

(a) Replace the *Crown Royal* with a cheaper whiskey, like *Early Times*
(b) Replace the toddler safety lock on the cabinet door
(c) Ask your son if he'd like to take a taxi down to the *Cheetah Lounge* and share a few shooters
(d) Search for children's Tylenol in the medicine cabinet—the boy's headed for one heckuva hangover

The answer is
(d). Now, I can understand, being a frugal father myself that (a) has a certain logic to it, but good whiskey should only be shared with your wife and good friends. (b) might seem plausible at first glance, but the first time toddlers unlatch safety latches is the last time they work. Save (c) for college graduation—a blessed celebration for all. (d) may not be ideal, but put the liquor out of reach, and you should be okay.

Question:

You're on solo parent patrol during a four-day Mommy-seminar. Your toddler's going on four, yet shrieks to share a bedtime bottle every night with her infant brother. Should you?

(a) Snatch your son's bottle away, making him wail louder than his sister
(b) Turn up the audio monitor, call Aunt Marcy and tell her the world is coming to an end
(c) Flip the wall switch on and off like a strobe light, yelling at the children, "Control yourselves or else!"
(d) Let sonny keep his milkie; give sweetie a ba-ba filled with wah-wah, then read a beddy-bye tale about moo-moo's before you pass out the binkies/pacies

The answer is
(d) again, of course. This has to be the easiest question/ answer ever given in history. If only high school and college had been this easy, huh? Answer (a) is ugly on any level, only an immature ding-dong would choose it, and that's not you. You're an important (and sometimes potent) pappy, and you know how bad dual-wailing can be. (b) is a cry for help of a different sort, and Marcy's already suspicious of your parenting abilities. No good. (c) = (a) + adds a third screaming voice—really stupid. Answer (d) is correct + cute, an unbeatable equation in your wife's eyes.

Question:

Your golden retriever's just had a litter. You open the closet door and find your recently weaned 18-month-old feasting with the puppies. Should you?

> (a) Close the closet door and pretend you didn't see him
> (b) Rush him to the emergency room for a rabies shot
> (c) Call your wife and tell her Sophie's litter's a little
>   larger than we thought
> (d) Yank your unfurry-faced son off the pile, slap his
>   paw, then bark at him, "no more *101 Dalmations*
>   videos! Plus next year's Westminster show is out!"

The answer is
(c). We might all be tempted by (a), but we're doggone daddies (to our children *and* our canines) and ignoring this situation is unfair to all of them. (b) is an over-the-top response, unnecessary and uncool. Besides, everyone knows goldens

don't bite. (d) is more overdone and shamelessly dramatic than (b)—wasted punishment on deaf ears. (c) is thoughtful and courteous, just don't tell Mommy *why* the litter's larger.

Question:

Your daughter dines on her booster seat in the breakfast booth with the greatest of ease while you clean the kitchen counter. You turn to face her and she hurls a mashed potato-encrusted sippy cup at your crotch. Should you?

> (a) Collapse on the kitchen floor, hugging yourself
> (b) Be glad you have softball practice today—you're already wearing a cup
> (c) Throw her a curve by saying, "C'mon, kid, is that all you've got?"
> (d) Roar like a lion, "Are you out of your mind, you little moron? Daddy made those mashed potatoes from scratch!"

The answer is
(b). This question doesn't explore weaning per se, but the incident beautifully demonstrates our toddlers' love-hate relationship with sippy cups. Go ahead, choose (a). What happens if your wife walks in? You'll live forever with the legacy of a wimp. (c) is unadulterated (and un-adult-like) taunting—save it for your next softball game. (d) misses the point entirely. This episode is about trading bottles for sippies; it's not about your dreams of culinary conquest. (b) is smart and shows how to be a prudent pappy...but if you donned your apron too, you'd be twice as smart and doubly protected.

Question:

Your wife is away on international business for 19 days when you set out for a stroll in the park with your sonny-buck. You're doing your best to set a great weaning example, but you find yourself staring at the big-breasted blonde on a bench. Should you?

> (a) Hold your head down and pick up the strolling pace
> (b) Quietly order, "Sam, look the other way—now."
> (c) Moan, "Oh, Sammy, I miss Mommy's num-nums more than you do!"
> (d) Cough and exclaim in a husky voice, "Samuel, balloons are so nice! How many would you like at your birthday party?"

The answer is
(d). If we were robots instead of men, (a) would win hands-down. Remember, weaning is a lifelong battle. (b)? Sure, as if your toddler's going to listen to quiet orders of any kind. (c) would be a rational and heartfelt response for any sensitive man in touch with his feelings...but as Mommy's right-hand man, you'd be setting a terrible example. (d) is best...letting you express yourself, plus exhibit your sense of planning and preparedness...fine illustrations of maturity for your toddler.

Question:

One hot summer day you and your daughter are on the sippy-cup shopping expedition from hell. Three malls, two flea markets and a USA Baby store later, she chooses a Winnie the Poohthemed sippy cup to be her very own. You breathe a sigh—it's the last such cup in inventory. She clutches it happily. Ecstatic, you open the car windows, then put Lillian in her booster seat. That's when you pull out of the parking lot and hear the sickening crunch under your right-front tire. Should you?

(a) Look in the rear view mirror hopefully and inquire, "Lilly, dear heart, is Winnie back there with you?"
(b) Fetch the destroyed cup off the boiling asphalt
(c) Scream, "Look at the tire marks across tigger's back—is that supposed to be artistic?"
(d) Bang your head on the sweaty steering wheel, then drive by the hardware store for duct tape

The answer is
(b). Don't let this one get you all worked up. Your damsel-in-distress had an itch; she put the cup down to scratch. These things happen. If you were Prince Charming wearing earplugs, you might have a reason to choose (a), but you'd end up with (b) anyway. (c) could help reinforce elements of Lilly's next arts & crafts playdate, but the tears might not stop for a week—who needs it? (d)? Well, you just spent seven hours searching for the perfect cup. Do you think a duct tape patch obliterating all of Pooh Corner will seal the deal?

END OF QUIZ

Whether you see yourself as a brilliant knight in shining armor, or a humble peasant too ignorant to be interrogated, we hope your test-taking experience was a pleasant one.

With adolescent dalliances in mind, many male parents have inflated expectations about their ability to score. They forget—adolescence is ancient history, both mentally and physically. Don't be confused. With little children, big mortgages, a dull lance and a set of armor that doesn't fit like it used to...you're in the dark ages of adulthood, now.

Nevertheless, get out your trusty abacus and count up how many questions you answered correctly. If you truly answered half or better, you're smarter than the average Sir Popsalot.

Score ten for each correct answer. Compare your results with other crusading weaners. Then, together, toast your fatherly-aptitudes with frothy tankards of mead!

Score	Crusading Class
0	Diseased Peasant
10	Brainless Serf
20	Court Jester
30	Tone-Deaf Minstrel
40	Scholar
50	Wizard
60	Noble Prince
70	Feudal Lord
80	*DRAGON SLAYER*

At the end of the day, whether it takes two weeks, two months or two years, your little infidel will have wised up and started slurping whole milk from nippleless containers. The journey from breast to bottle to plastic cup to stemmed goblet passes through a swirl of confusing roadblocks, detours and dead-ends.

But you and your adoring toddler will reach the Promised Land of Weaners in due time.

No weenie, you. After your daring deeds and chivalrous crusades in the name of weaning, you'll have time to rest. You and Toddler. Just you two...together. In a golden land of milk and honey, sweetly pouring without a breast or bottle in sight to tempt either of you.

Chapter six

A Snotty Attitude Toward the Common Cold

For better for worse, for richer for poorer,
for sickness and in health...
till Mommy us do part—

(from *The Book of Common Prayer*
with a slight alteration)

⌐   ⌐   ⌐   ⌐   ⌐   ⌐   ⌐

As a caring Daddy earning your diploma in toddler doctoring, you'll soon discover the true genius of the person way back when who hit the bullseye when she dubbed it the *common* cold. Boy, they weren't kidding around about kids and colds. Especially if your Todd or Toddette is enrolled in day care, you can expect constant battles with infectious marauders.

[105]

And we're just talking about the other toddlers in the room. The germs themselves are a whole different story—a topic not blessed with a happy ending, in case you wondered.

So Let's Quit Kidding Around About Toddlers and Colds

Don't bother trying to locate a child care center light-years' cleaner and more sanitary than the rest. They all have their good days and bad days. Just like you and your toddler.

Imagine if you cared for 20 to 30 younguns at your home five days a week. You could employ dozens of maids and sanitation engineers and it wouldn't prevent the germs from doing their dirty work. I mean, germs and toddlers go together like ice cream and cake, beer and pretzels or boo-boos and band-aids.

You just can't have one without the other. Not for more than a day or two, anyway. When it comes to toddlers, you can bathe 'em, scrub 'em, spray 'em or bubble-wrap 'em. You can wash his chubby hands till he squeals. The germs will still find a way to dance the night away inside your toddler's immune system.

Now if every young person at every playground had his hands scoured on the hour, you might make some headway. But the fact is, you can't wash 'em all and you can't watch 'em all. No wonder day care is notorious. All those pairs of hands and pudgy little digits digging into places they shouldn't go. Picking up squirting secretions here, sticky fluids there, hardened crud everywhere...then passing their findings along to toddler-neighbors down the length of the lunch table. It's enough to make you sick.

The irony of it is, finally, the concept of sharing is catching on—in the most catching way possible! That's when the cold takes hold and the cute button nose begins to drip...drip...drip. Once it starts, there's no way to muzzle the mucous...the viral invaders will camp out in the caverns of your toddler's cranium as long as they please.

Of course, with your luck, the cold suddenly reigns supreme on a rainy afternoon pick-up from your favorite day care academy—and you-know-who is in solo command for the upcoming weekend.

Irony is everywhere. You head home to your apartment, driving in the cold November rain, evidence of a cold front slashing through your state, a prelude to the season's first true cold snap. You take your nose-trickling toddlerette by her germy little hand and walk into the cold foyer. Your friendly beagle gives you the cold shoulder; the siamese gives you a cold stare. You press your stubbled cheek against your child's forehead and feel a fever just beginning.

You break out into a cold sweat.

Saturday noon. You're swimming upstream in a river of snot. It's everywhere. Slippery palm prints on the rubber tree plant. Rivulets of mucus creating new patterns all over your Oriental rug. Globs of phlegm covering the high chair tray. Pure green hockers on your favorite lambswool sweater. Smears of sputum vibrating across the television screen.

You've emptied three boxes of tissues and taken out the kitchen garbage twice. The "big-person" potty in your daughter's bathroom is stopped up with tissue residue. You've wiped her nose 84 times since breakfast—still you can't keep up with the nostril torrent.

How could such a cute little pug produce such an incredible discharge?

You feel sorry for the way she feels, but unfortunately, you're beginning to feel even sorrier for yourself. You won't be relieved from toddler duty for at least 32 hours. But already you're getting sick of it and sick from it in more ways than you can count.

What should you do?
1) Pack up your sweet little honey-bunny (and your twin-colds), jump in the car and spread the ill-fated news all over town
2) Huddle together around the medication inhaler, wrapped in blankets like Eskimos in an igloo
3) Call Mommy—blubber, snivel and cry
4) Take massive doses of Robutussin and Nyquil till you both pass out

The answer? NONE OF THE ABOVE.

None of these answers is a positive choice for confident father-protectors in command of Toddlerville action. These are simply the types of cop-outs that Loser Dads from

Loser Town contemplate. So, if you can't get hold of the cold, at least get hold of yourself.

Consider a few of these professional tips compiled by experienced 20th century toddler-fathers who pioneered common cold protocol for all us New Millennium rookies. Some of them are based on pure common sense. Others don't make any sense at all. It makes you think some of the interviewed dads were downright delirious. Can't blame them though.

That's what happens when the fever gets you.

Cold Season Do's and Dont's
(for *Wise Guys* like you and me)

Not only are you earning your degree as a toddler-intern, I know you, like any hero, are yearning to make a healthy showing in the sick rooms of toddler town. So catch a few of these time-honored tips before you catch something not so nice. Like toddler-contracted mononucleosis, for instance.

DO get out and get some healthy fresh air, even if you can't take it in through your nose

DON'T stay cooped up inside passing germs back and forth like a (sick) game of table tennis

DO take a soft-spoken, sympathetic attitude toward your ailing little one

DON'T scream, "I hate you, you snot-nosed little dweeb!"

DO pretend you're Doctor Kildare for a day...the well-groomed, up-and-coming resident with a healthy attitude and a ready answer for every cold-natured dilemma

DON'T parade around in a zebra-skin sarong like a witch doctor holding a spear, singing, "Ooo-eee, ooo-ah-ah, ting-tang, walla-walla bing-bang, ooo-eee, ooo-ah-ah, ting-tang, walla-walla bing-bang."

DO serve up steaming bowls of chicken soup and be sure your toddler breathes in the healthful vapors while she eats

DON'T slap her on the back, holding her head down over the bowl until she sucks in broth through her nasal passages

DO use a rubber bulb syringe, like a gentle nurse-in-training, to suction out mucus from the flowing shnozzola, at least twice an hour

DON'T hook up a portable Dirt Devil, like a barnstorming cowboy, then run it across her face, exclaiming, "Don't worry, Little Darlin'. If'n this don't work, we'll bring out the wet-vac and let 'er rip!"

DO politely inquire of your child's primary day care attendant, if the premise's hand-washing policy is clear-cut and up-to-date, according to 21st century standards

DON'T descend on the day care facility with a pack of personal-injury attorneys, claiming, "We know what you're up to, you dirty freaks—and we'll make you pay!"

DO sit with daughter-dear in the bathroom while you run a hot shower for 15-20 minutes, letting her inhale invigorating steam to help alleviate clogged airways

DON'T pack her up and take her to a men's fitness club steam room for a traumatizing experience sitting next to fat-rippled 50-year-old men with too-small towels draped about them

DO visit the playground and traipse into the women's bathroom every fifteen minutes for dual hand-washing, and especially, hand-washing instruction—both with the antibacterial soap you've thoughtfully brought along

DON'T stick around when the women in the stalls start screaming at you to get out

DO spend a fortune on the latest technology in thermometers, such as a split-second/super-duper/tympanic/lithium battery digital readout ear-scan model

DON'T buy an old-fashioned mercury-filled rectal thermometer—and if you already have one, don't stick it anywhere except in a time capsule.

DO call your pediatrician and wake him up at 2:30 a.m. when your toddler's audio fever monitor sounds its alarm and the digital ear-scan readout exceeds 98.6-degrees fahrenheit

DON'T be surprised when he tells you those new-fangled ear thermometers are unreliable and he won't budge from his warm bed until you fetch the rectal device and earn your reading the old-fashioned way

[111]

DO accept your Aunt Myrtle's invitation to drop off your sickly toddler-dear at her house so that you can have a fun afternoon attending the international auto show

DON'T accept auntie's suggestion that she cruise over in her souped-up Ford jalopy and spend the weekend with the two of you wiping brows, whipping up porridge and watching NASCAR on TV

DO set up a cool-mist vaporizer in your son's room to help soothe his wheezing

DON'T hook up a hose to the corner fire hydrant and spray-blast his daybed, chortling, "I'll drown those damn germs!"

DO take a nap when your toddler is breathing freely enough to take one, because you both need the rest, and also because you can dream about being a wise, heroic tough-guy with a nickname like *The Germinator*

DON'T mention your dreams to anyone

⌐   ⌐   ⌐   ⌐   ⌐

Your Toddler's Infectious Personality

If you're a father with a fetish for clean; if you get a tad freaked-out by a double-barreled dose of grubby, grimy toddler-filth, then you may want to apply for a transfer of duty. 'Cause Daddy, you're about to get germinated, from the ground up.

Put simply, your toddler's never met a germ she didn't like. You might think that's a sick attitude, but the feeling is one of mutual admiration. Germs instinctively know your kid is a first-class carrier, a prime agent at any age, but one they exhibit a special affection for at toddler-time.

Your battle against germs is Cold War at its finest...boring, unfair, frustrating and full of disappointments—just like the 1950s.

But back to the present. As far as germs are concerned, your 30-month-old lass is what you might call a site for sore eyes. She's the hostess with the mostest. One who sends out frequent invitations to party-hardy. A popular place to go with a large group of friends when you want to get down with your bad germ-self.

As the male-formulated half of the parenting prescription, you already know, once the revelry starts, the germs won't stop till the party reaches a fever-pitch. And guess what? The guest list sports a very diverse makeup. Plus, these germs come cloaked in a variety of disguises so you can't always

[113]

recognize them easily. Some say, over 200 different types of viral visitors can come calling. And every one of these ambassadors of the common cold is uncommonly well-equipped to make your little girl miserable.

Then one day you finally close the party down and throw out the no-good germ-bums who came courting your daughter. Finally, you even manage to get rid of the sniffles.

That's when you'll be beset by a new cold-related menace, such as the evil, triple-threat, head-attacking trifecta known as ear infection, strep throat and pink eye.

Sick as a Dog and Nowhere to Flee

A Tale of Woe from a Dog-Faced
Veteran of the Toddler-Care Trenches

Colds are commonplace, that much we know. Pray tell, how easy life would be if that were the only common sickness we pappys had to confront.

Want to strike fear into the hearts of even the bravest toddler-fathers? Just mention the term *flu season* to a crowd of daddies. Watch them scatter and duck like cowards in retreat, hiding under desks and behind plants, wailing dire warnings such as, "Incoming!" and "Fire in the Hole!" and "Hit the Deck!" and "The Redcoats are Coming!"

If you announce in a loud voice, *False Alarm!* or *All Clear!* most of the rehabilitated vets will come out of hiding and even carry on a conversation, if your questioning is gentle and non-threatening.

One weathered-looking dad with a tick in his cheek and a limp to his gait even agreed to have his recollections recorded if we could grant him anonymity.

Here's what the poor guy had to say...

Simon (not his real name): *It was last winter; Sarah was two-and-a-half. Mommy was visiting her mother in the country. Friday night, we shared pizza in the breakfast nook—everything was fine. Then Sarah coughed and said her throat hurt.*

"Twoat hoit, Dadd-ee. Not swawwoe." She looked up at me with wide blue eyes, pinched her neck and grimaced.

I picked her up and sat her on the kitchen counter. I touched her forehead with the back of my hand and felt the warmth. I noticed her flushed, pink cheeks and ran for the digital thermometer. It took me several squirming minutes to keep it under her tongue long enough to get a reading.

100.5 degrees.

The freezer held a few banana popsicles. I got one and broke it in half and gave it to my little girl.

"Hold it over the sink," I said.

"I achy, too, Dadd-ee." Sarah yawned and rubbed her eye with one hand, popsicle tipping and dripping in the other.

Have you ever thought about how this stuff always happens when you're totally unprepared? I felt like a grunt sitting in a foxhole, under fire, but with very little ammunition. But at least I had a few more popsicles.

I also had Children's Motrin and frozen orange juice. I dispensed the former and mixed up the latter. Before I gave her the O.J., it was time to check her temperature again.

102˚.

My wife had taught me about keeping a chart. She told me it's just like in the birthing suite when you're timing the contractions. Get the reading, then write it down.

Right. The next number I wrote? 102.5˚.

By the time the doctor called back it was 103°.

He told me to keep doing what I was doing. If the fever hadn't gone down by tomorrow afternoon, he'd call in an anti-viral prescription.

Now Sarah had chills and aches, so I wrapped her up and held her. In between, I kept plying her with fruit juices. We went to the potty eight times before bedtime.

The Motrin kept the fever at 103° or below. Grateful, I decided to sleep on the rug by her crib. At least I tried to. Sarah kept waking up and crying...her throat hurt, her tummy hurt, her head hurt. I gave her a sippy cup with more juice, but the chills came back and her hands shook so badly she couldn't hold it.

I picked her up, held her in the rocking chair and held the cup so she could drink. Somehow, we went to sleep in that position, with the sippy cup oozing cranberry juice over the pocket of my white dress shirt.

Next morning, fever the same, we woke the doc early and headed for the drug store. It would take the anti-viral drugs some time to take effect. In the meantime, I made Jell-o. Unfortunately, Sarah's headache, throat ache and chills got worse.

She spent most of midday Saturday leaning over a puke pan and crying. We called Mommy and she told us what a good job we were doing, helping each other feel better when times were tough. We said thanks, but we have to go now.

Uh-huh. Go is right.

The diarrhea hit soon after. The fever spiked along late afternoon. I kept forcing the liquids and Sarah kept sending them back out, top to bottom. I couldn't keep up with the mess because my first job was to keep her comfortable. At least, that was the goal. The mess was spreading room to room, bath to bed to den. The place looked like hell—but Sarah and I looked worse.

Kept checking the temp. It wasn't getting any better, but it wasn't getting any worse. 102°-103°. I took that as a positive, plus Sarah's stomach eased up on her, even if the aches and chills didn't.

We spent the night again in the rocking chair, together with the sippy cup dribbles and caking diarrhea.

By morning, the fever had eased a notch or two. By early afternoon, Sarah kept down some soup and Jell-o and I think she even smiled once. Around 3:00, Mommy walked in the front door and I smiled too. Then I went to the bathroom, looked in the mirror and practically scared myself. I looked like a bearded scarecrow who lived in a garbage dump.

Sarah was definitely better—but I was getting worse. Fever and chills and a sweaty mattress were mine, all mine, for the next four days. I missed a week of work and lost 16 pounds. I drink Ensure *noon and night, but I've only gained six back.*

Back at work, I tried to concentrate, but couldn't. My boss sent me to the clinic, but I caught a different strain of flu from a fellow employee and missed another 10 days of work.

I lost my job. My wife divorced me. Because I'm unemployed, the judge gave Sarah's mother sole custody.

My ex-wife won't let Sarah see me because she's afraid our little girl will get sick again. I live with my mother now. She's been very good to me (Simon sighs.) *I plan to get back on my feet again, real soon.*

I just have this overwhelming fear of touching doorknobs. It makes finding a job very difficult....

After your experience, would you have any specific advice for our readers?

Simon: *Get your toddler's flu shot in October. Every year they say it's a different strain. It might not help, but it might.*

Anything else before you go?

Simon (limping away, face twitching): *Stock your pantry like it's a bomb shelter. Stock your medicine cabinet like it's a hospital. Don't let your child out of the house from November to April. Don't let your wife go away—ever. Keep your strength up...don't let the evil virus get you down. Don't give up...never give in. Don't let the flu bug ruin your life forever.*

Simon, thank you.

Simon (shuffling off): *Sure.*

⌐   ⌐   ⌐   ⌐   ⌐

Simon Says: Beware of the Bug!

Cold Snap Tool Tips
for Cool Poppa Docs

The best advice we can give you is don't let Simon's sad story happen to you. You have to be cool during cold and flu season. That means being smarter than the average polar bear pater. That means, during the dark days of winter, you need to be prepared like the bright Papa you are.

Battling attacking germ hordes demands a bloated arsenal of clever tools and techniques. So keep your pantry, cabinets, garage and sick-bay bunker stuffed with the following essentials. As a frontline father armed to the teeth, you'll be ready to leap into the fray the second the enemy's close enough to see your toddler's white blood cells.

Remember. When it comes to germ warfare, anything's fair. So buckle up your gas mask, strap a fruit-juice canteen to your ammunition belt and jump into the brawl. Who knows. You might make a name for yourself overnight in the fight against fever. Gaining fame, rising in rank faster than legions of fathers before you...your name could echo across toddlerville valleys far and wide.

You. The Hero. The Legend. The Chosen One. The Daddy known as the courageous, caped super-hero germ-destroyer on a desperate mission to save the toddler world.

The one-and-only, Kung-Flu Fighter!

Make copies and post this list of toddler/sick-bay essentials in several prominent places. *(For example, inside your refrigerator, on the back side of your medicine cabinet door, next to your toddler's crib/daybed, and over the workbench in your garage.)*

If your wife laughs at you for going to extremes, flip your cape casually over one shoulder and say, "Dear, dear, dear. Please do not attempt to distract me. I am on a mission. I am a legend in my own mind. And I also know what happened to Simon. Hah!"

Item	Purpose
Vitamin C	*prevention*
Q-Tip	*swabbing*
Bedpan	*up-chucking*
Microscope	*spying on the enemy*
20-gallon tubs	*storing anti-bacterial soap*
Digital thermometer	*checking toddler temps*
5-gallon tubs	*storing chicken soup*
Nasal aspirator	*suction*
Wet-Dry vac	*suction*
Graph paper	*charting toddler temps*
Soft-tip meds dispenser	*for toddler*
Easy-pour liquor flask	*for father*
Cool mist vaporizer	*unclogging toddler airways*

Item	Purpose
Hi-pressure fire hose	*scouring toddler sick-bays*
Children's Tylenol	*toddler dose*
Aleve	*daddy dose*
Flashlight	*check temp of sleeping toddler*
Flares	*light way for doctor's arrival*
Pacifier	*soothing toddler*
Stress ball	*soothing father*
Remote fever monitor	*alerting parent*
Police siren	*alerting neighborhood*
Rocking chair	*grab-a-wink-for-two*
Good night's sleep	*for no one*
Boxcar full of tissues	*swiping toddler nostrils*
Driveway dumpster	*discarding toddler tissues*
Bathtub	*comforting toddler*
Pond	*drowning father*

⌐ ⌐ ⌐ ⌐ ⌐

Pop's Recipe for
Sick-Bay Success

Taking care of ill-tempered toddlers is challenge enough. We have way too much respect for fellow father-caretakers to end a chapter with a series of sick jokes. You deserve positive counsel in an uncomplicated, stress-free format.

Here you can serve yourself an extra helping of solid toddler-care advice designed to fill the appetite of even the hungriest, hero-aspiring poppa doc.

Les Enfant Infirmité Garnished with Fièvre and Misère

——serves two——

—Ingredients—

• one germ-induced toddler, cleaned, dried and prepared for doctoring   • 1 tsp of ibuprofen, liquefied   • 10 lbs of tissue, not shredded   • 1 pinch of nose, for blowing
• 2 cups chicken *potage* for slurping   • 3 cups cognac *pour papa*   • 1 ramekin of Jell-o, finely chopped
• 1 jar of Vicks Vapo-Rub, softened at room temperature

[125]

- 1 zesty mucus squeeze, boiled till syrupy, then congealed
- 15 garlic cloves, thinly sliced, wrapped in bouquet garni

—Preparation—

1. Wash doctor-cook's hands thoroughly in anti-bacterial soap. Dry thoroughly. Wash fevered toddler's hands thoroughly in anti-bacterial soap. Dry thoroughly. Repeat on the quarter-hour.

2. Heat a small saucepan and prepare to make the Jell-o.

3. Pour a snifter of cognac and serve it to yourself. Drink a portion, according to your symptoms.

4. Serve the ibuprofen to your toddler as an appetizer.

5. Open hotel-size box of tissue, peel off a few layers, approach your toddler, pinch and blow.

6. Wash both pairs of hands once again in pre-heated tap water.

7. Check contents of cognac snifter, drink to taste.

8. Stir Jell-o; open can of Campbells chicken broth or chicken & stars soup. Heat in microwave for approximately 2:30 minutes.

9. Finely chop multiple garlic cloves, wrap & tie in cheese cloth.

10. Serve chicken soup to toddler, allow Jell-o to cool in freezer.

—Recipe Preparation—
(continued)

11. Drain contents of snifter.

12. After several minutes with face over soup bowl, toddler's nose will run like a wide receiver. Prepare to capture bountiful mucus sampling as second dessert ingredient. Squeeze gently—yet thoroughly— like a Napoli lemon.

13. Add cornstarch, reduce mucus squeeze to syrup consistency.

13. Check Vicks Vapo-Rub for consistent softness.

14. Check contents of newly poured snifter for consistent taste.

15. Serve Jell-o.

16. Drain snifter.

17. Your toddler is full. No need for second dessert. Capture the syrupy reduction in a plastic bowl and freeze it. Later, when you're both well again, you can carve the hardened mucus into a beautiful ice sculpture...the perfect toddler table decoration to remind the two of you how much you care about (and for) each other.

18. Just a touch more cognac as a nightcap.

19. Stagger to bathroom with toddler in tow for final hand-washing of the evening. Rub toddler's chest with Vick's. If your offspring hates the rubdown and blubbers about it, swing the stringed

bouquet garni pouch above his face and say, "Sorry, son. It's either Vick's or the garlic. Take your pick."

20. Check toddler's temperature one last time before nite-nite. Use the digital thermometer from the bathroom *NOT* the poke-n-probe turkey thermometer from the kitchen oven.

21. Flop in the rocking chair with the last of your snifter, slur your way through Mother Goose till you both fall asleep.

TIME: approximately one-hour twenty-five minutes dependent upon your stove (gas or electric), the size of your brandy snifter, and whether your toddler has a simple cold or the flu.

COOK'S TIP: though you want to make a memorable presentation, for this meal it is acceptable to use plastic tableware. But keep the floral decoration real (even if you can't smell it).

VARIATION: substitute acetaminophen for ibuprofen if you prefer.

SERVING IDEA: sprinkle generously Herbes de Provence and costly (but colorful) saffron across your toddler's chest to complement the adhesive qualities of the special rub. *Magnifique!*

Chapter seven

Lullabies, Cries and Bloodshot Zombie Eyes

Do not go gentle into that good night...
rage, rage against the dying of the light

—Dylan Thomas

⌐   ⌐   ⌐   ⌐   ⌐   ⌐   ⌐

Mommy is out with the girls. Her best friend's younger sister is getting married and the bachelorette party is at a strip joint called *First Class Male*. You've read 12 nursery rhymes to your two-and-a-half-year-old and she's wide awake watching you fall asleep. You know it's past bedtime but you haven't had the heart to take her down the hall because your little girl misses her mommy and so do you.

Speaking of heart, your esophagus suddenly sprouts a flame from the off-brand frozen pot pies you and your little one shared for dinner. Good. Not only did you convince your toddler to actually *share* something, but the heartburn will keep you awake long enough to start a new story, then put her to bed properly. Very good. Only now, thinking about the rollicking entertainment at the *First Class Male* is making your indigestion worse, so you'd better wrap up *Peter Rabbit* and reach for a *Rolaids*.

Now, finally, it's time to lead your lovely toddlerette down the hallway to her bedroom. Head down and shuffling, like a death-row convict marching to the guillotine, your sweet, used-to-be baby looks at you as if you're the hooded executioner.

You slip into the toddler-room rocking chair with your prisoner and agree to her final request for a few minutes of *Jailhouse Rock*. With ba-ba in hand, dispensing unwanted weaning-water instead of lip-smacking cow's milk, you creak your way to slumber.

That is, until Miss Kitty slips into the room and gets her fat tail caught under the rocker leg.

YEEEOOOWWW! Screech! What a racket!

Miss Kitty scrambles across the rug and out the door before you crunch her tail again. Melissa's heavy head jerks forward, eyes popped wide-open, the drowsy mood of a moment ago now seems time-zones away.

[130]

What can a toddler-dad do now?

You plod right back to square one, that's what. You get out Mother Goose, open her up to *Winken, Blinken and Nod*, and you start reading. Because that's just about what you would wish for if someone would ask you.

A little more Nod, and a lot less Winking and Blinking from that sweet toddler face in the crook of your arm.

Don't Rock the Boat— or the Cradle

In case you had any doubt about it, a rocking chair makes a very smart addition to any toddler's room. Until they get to be heavyweights—in the 35 to 40 pound range—you can rock in comfort and safety. After that, you can suffer permanent damage to abdominal muscles, knee joints, achilles tendons, and worst of all for dads, the groin area.

The rocking chair is also a metaphor for toddler-sleep strategy. The rocker represents a soothing, repetitive motion to lull the little maniacs into a false sense of snooziness. That's the trick. Literally, you need to bore your toddler out of her skull with a mind-numbing routine that never varies. Just like the rocking chair, you repeat the same motions over and over and over till your brainwashed tot gives in, pushed gently over the rim of the sleep canyon.

So rock all you care to in a graceful spindle-backed or

old-fashioned straw-backed rocking chair. But don't rock any-thing else. Always remember—when there's a toddler on board...

> *Never rock the* habit *boat* and
> *Never tip the* routine *canoe.*

Otherwise, you could end up with...

> a *night owl* past midnight or
> a *day snoozer* past noon.

Working parents like us don't need either of the above. Neither do siblings, *in* utero or out, your visiting relatives, favorite pets, au pairs, playdate companions, day-nannies, or day care personnel. Nobody, but nobody loves a cranky, nap-less, sleep-deprived toddler—no matter how lovable they are normally. That is, if normal is a word you can associate with toddlers in the first place.

So get with a bedtime routine, establish it, then stick with it until hell freezes over. Any other pappy-approach and you'll not have a snowball's chance of having a happy toddler-homelife.

How do you unwrap a routine? Swing a little of your under-appreciated, under-utilized male logic into action. (I understand it's hard to stay sharp in the logic department when you're dealing with toddlers, the most illogical humans on the planet except for their teenage counterparts.) But try to get back in touch with your tried-and-true, logical self.

Think about things that make you drowsy as an adult.

No—you needn't include such things as ice cream & cake, sex, scotch & soda, funny cigarettes and/or pipes, cigars, late-night television, over-the-counter sleep aids or PTA meetings. Your toddler is not ready for any of these items, except the first, and that should be reserved only for daytime birthday parties.

We're talking about more innocent adult delicacies that you probably take for granted. Like a nice hug. A soothing bath. A warm glass of milk. A cuddle. A dimly lit room. A quiet conversation that makes you smile, not laugh. A clean, comfortable pair of jammies. A small snack that gives you a contented tummy—not an overstuffed, sugar-coated belly accompanied by an over-active bladder.

Example of a GOOD bedtime routine:

—taking a warm bath

—putting on clean, comfortable jammies (right style for the season)

—eating a light snack

—brushing those toothies

—turning down the lights and the noise

—talking a little about events of the day (but avoiding grand discussions of tomorrow's plans— toddlers tend to get too excited and too worked up about anything futuristic)

—saying good night (keep it short...limit the ritual to living people and pets within the home. Exclude your neighbor's cat, favorite stuffed animals (*that* could take all evening), houseplants, toys and portraits of ancient—or remote—family members)

—reading a bedtime story (toddler gets to choose...but nothing too dramatic or too funny)

—singing a lullaby (try it yourself or offer up a recording of Mommy. Another musical idea is to play soft, soothing music in the background while you read...try light classical or perhaps environmental sounds such as ocean waves, gentle raindrops or distant waterfalls)

—tucking toddler in affectionately (the exact, same way every night, without a hint of variation)

Example of a BAD bedtime routine:

—wetting down your front lawn till it's muddy, inviting over all of your daughter's playmates, then refereeing a hard-fought game of toddler-rugby after dark

—telling your son, "Forget the p.j.'s, bub. You can sleep nude under an electric blanket, like ol' Dad

—wolfing down a dozen Krispy Kreme doughnuts, washed down with a liter of Pepsi

—telling your daughter, "Honey, I wouldn't worry your pretty head about dental care. You'll see. The Tooth Fairy's gonna pay you lots of visits and snatch out those little baby teeth by the time you're eight or nine"

—constructing a fluorescent shop light over your son's crib, saying, "Hey, if it's good for the fish, it's good for you"

—turning his portable stereo up to Volume 9 and slipping in a CD, *The Best of John Philip Sousa*

—starting a tirade about the miserable day you had at work, then going on about how you'd like to kill your boss if you could get away with it and not end up in the state penitentiary until your toddler-daughter is middle-aged

—smiling afterward, then asking your daughter, "How was your day, honey?"

[135]

—taking your son around to every nook & cranny in your home to bid *bon soir* to all of the unappreciated insects. Finally, digging up a healthy glob of nightcrawlers from the backyard, dumping them in your son's lap, imploring, "Say *nite-nite* to the Squirmy Wormies, too!"

—kicking off your nightly reading with a couple of choice ghost stories, chased by two or three discreet passages from *Red Dragon* by Thomas Harris, and *The Pit and The Pendulum* by Edgar Allan Poe

—plugging in a microphone to the top of the toddler stereo, before announcing, "It's Karaoke Time!" Then ripping into a tuneful rendition of *Chicago (That Toddlin' Town)*

—keeping the microphone, then leaning over for a forehead kiss and head pat before announcing, "Introducing tonight's special mystery guest for your nightmare pleasure, from behind closet door number two, it's Mr. Monster!"

⌐   ⌐   ⌐   ⌐   ⌐

Above all, whichever ritual you select, you should remember to approach it with a lively, toddler-centric brain filled with old-fashioned daddy-logic. That is, you need to think fast, but act slow. Leap ahead mentally, but plod along physically. Talk in a soft, flat monotone as much as possible (like the history professor whose name you can't remember).

Think dull, stale, tiresome, monotonous thoughts. Make frequent references to how sleepy everyone gets this time of night. Close your eyes and yawn a lot.

When all is said and done, bedtime tactics revolve around a very simple equation. Dads from Arizona to Tanzania rely on the same formula for sleepytime success:

$$\text{Routine} = \text{Serene}$$
$$+$$
$$\text{Boring} = \text{Snoring}$$

Now, we've had a couple of rogue reports from desperate toddler-dads who've arrived at a different sort of formula for inducing bedtime slumber. It's called hypnotism.

One father, up past midnight 43 days in a row, borrowed an old book on the subject from his grandfather's library. He followed the steps and said they worked the first time out. Possible? Sure. But we're guessing they both fell asleep from exhaustion. Consequently, we can't sanction the advice.

Anyway, for the record, here's what Hypnotist Pop said:

[137]

Go through each step of the infernal bedtime routine. Get your toddler as relaxed as can be in his crib. Tell him you're trying out a new parenting role as Doctor Hippo the Hypnotist. Tell him this'll be fun. Tell him not to worry if he can't remember anything about it tomorrow—that's the fun part.

Beforehand, when you borrow the book, also borrow your grandfather's pocket watch. Get in position over your resting toddler in the crib. Get close, but not too close. Hold the gold pocket watch over his head and dangle it a while. Then slowly swish the watch back and forth at the end of the chain. Watch your toddler's eyes follow the face of the watch. Tick-tick-tick.

Say things like, "You're getting sleepy, little buddy. Very, very sleepy." Keep swishing the glittering watch sideways above your youngster's face. Let its shadow swoop side to side over his face. Watch your toddler's eyes get heavy. Very, very heavy.

Soon, your own eyes will probably get heavy. Guard against falling asleep yourself and collapsing in a heap over the crib railing. Gold watches tend to be heavy and might bruise your youngun if dropped from a height of more than 10 inches.

If the spell doesn't take the first night, try it again the second. Then try again a third. If hypnotism doesn't work after a week, give the watch and book back to your grandfather and go back to the cursed ritual you were trying previously. But don't complain to your grandpap. Just remember, back in his day, they may not have had satellite TV and info-mercials, but there were still quacks aplenty.

The Crying Game

You're a master of logic. A man in touch with the toddler psyche on every level, subconscious and conscious. You have meticulously developed a nighttime routine as slick as any *Saturday Night Live* performer in history. Yet, whenever Mommy leaves town, the very first night, your clean routine collapses like a cheap circus tent. Behind your back, all down the block, toddlers are laughing at your botched-up bedtime bungling. And their Mommies? They're laughing too.

What a joke.

The problem is your toddler. (Gee, what a revelation.) Not that she's abnormal. She's just decided to apply a little lung power to her protests about Mommyless bedtime. You worked the routine to perfection. You read the ideal nite-nite tale. The warm bath? Ah, nothing less than luxurious and languorous. A gourmet snack followed the tub, an incredible blend of cookie sweetness without excessive sugar. Brilliant! Quietly, under a dim nightstand lamp (you cleverly changed the bulb from 75- to 40-watts earlier) you talked of the day's playdate activities. The whole while, your voice a delicate treasure of monotoned blandness.

After nite-nite waves and kisses blown to Nanna and Pap-Pap's pictures on the wall, you execute a polished tuck-in with kisses light as cotton candy, followed by head-pats so feathery-soft her angel-hair ringlets shifted nary a millimeter.

You leave the cribside on gossamer wings, as light on your feet as a man can possibly be. Confirming the night-light's friendly glow, you ease the bedroom door closed without a breath of sound. You've just danced your way through the season's perfect sleep ballet, and all of your critics are snoring.

Three steps down the hallway, a bloodcurdling cacophony erupts with a ferocity you thought reserved for medieval torture chambers. No. The sound rises to new pinnacles, then clabbers down steps of gurgling sobs as if disappearing into the recesses of a chasm. Then roaring back, flowing out the mouth of the cave and soaring again—now screeching—like some wretched, wounded bird of prey. A prehistoric, winged creature, perhaps.

Like something from the animal kingdom, anyway.

You think, how could that be my daughter's cry? Three minutes ago so peaceful and cherubic, innocence under down. That's a voice not from within that face. Or chest. Those lungs. That shy mouth. Not that sound. Not my daughter.

Then you open the door and she stands at the end of the crib buckling with spasms of grief. Gushing tears. Screaming pain. Pooping in the pants. Total loss of control.

Worse yet, she screams the immortal scream all toddler's scream. *"MOMMY! MOMMY! MOMMY!"* The rhythm might vary, but the cry comes in triplets, usually wrapped up prior to a louder, single version with a subject and verb. Such as, "I WANT *MOMMY!"*

You comfort her. You console. You quiet the beast within. But you can't be Mommy. All you can do is do the best you can to make Mommy proud when she returns. When she does, there's a strategy you might engage to win *The Crying Game* the next time you're alone and your toddler starts. Perhaps if she gets used to having you tuck her in with Mommy around, she won't snap so quickly when Mommy isn't.

I know. It's painful to hear, but volunteer more often for routine bedtime employment, and you can bank on an easier getaway down the line. Think of it as making deposits into a savings account. Extra bedtime duty now will pay handsome dividends later.

Whatever you do, don't let your toddler cry you into submission. Regular crying bouts aren't the same as tantrums, true. But you need to keep your guard up and counterpunch properly or you'll likely get knocked out in the early rounds.

In other words, let the screamer wail. For a bit, anyway. As with tantrums, you can't use sleep tools on toddlers such as REWARD, BRIBERY OR PUNISHMENT. Soothe and console, give a quick hug, but don't give in. Get earplugs instead.

Most of all, never feed a nighttime crier, emotionally or physically. Stay neutral. Maintain the monotone. And just because they look a little like cute, chubby hobbits, you can't feed him every time a toddler gets upset. Hobbits like double breakfasts and late-night sweet cakes on the menu. But your toddler doesn't have furry feet (we hope), and he doesn't need the sugary calories.

⌐   ⌐   ⌐   ⌐   ⌐

Singing the Bedtime Blues: a Note on Lullabies

You're a man. You're proud. You're an excellent father (most of the time) and you want to do the right thing. You know how much babies and toddlers love a mommy's voice. From her, they love to hear a lullaby more than they love to eat chocolate cake. Well, almost. But very possibly, you believe the lullaby is a square block in the round hole of your parenting pegboard. You believe, as a father, that you're able to carry out the garbage farther than you can carry a tune.

Well, in a classic, down-to-earth, bluesy way, a couple of incredibly talented, musical brothers of ours said it best,

"It Ain't Necessarily So!"

The truth is, you don't have to be a brilliant composer or lyricist to lullaby your toddler into posing as a peaceful sleeping beauty. You don't have to know opera. You don't need to be a booming Italian baritone (in fact it's better if you're not). You might be a tender Irish tenor who makes women weep— but you don't have to be. The fact is, you don't even have to sing to get the lullaby across.

As documented in *Keeping the Baby Alive till Your Wife Gets Home*, you can be a tone-deaf dud of a dad and still be a good hummer. All you have to do is get the melody going. Be gentle. Be melodic. Don't be embarrassed. Ask your wife for tone and lyric tips. She may raise an eyebrow, but she'll be happy to help you out.

[142]

Then, after weeks pass and you're finally alone, you can take the bedtime stage and croon a tune your toddler can't resist. Or hum. Your bygone babycakes won't care either way. Before you know it, your sweet paternal notes will cause his eyelashes to flutter and his lids to droop. Soon your toddler audience will nod its approval.

In no time, you'll be far from the toddler bedroom both physically and mentally. Settled in your leather easy chair with the brandy snifter at your elbow, *Porgy and Bess* playing (softly) on the family room stereo, and the Churchill Dominican glowing long, white ashes in crystal by the humidor...you can say aloud (but not too loud) to the serene, Mommyless household, "Cigar smoke? What cigar smoke?"

Everything You Know about Toddler Sleep You Learned with Bloodshot Zombie Eyes

Life is full of surprises.

Life with your toddler may be bizarre, predictable, rewarding, humiliating, shrill, shy, easy, hard, happy or sad. And those are just a sampling of the emotions you feel during breakfast. Which means, when the two of you are alone for a whole day, the possible emotional swings can only be described as indescribable.

Regardless, at the end of the long day, as endless as it may seem, bedtime is still a special time for the two of you. You know it's special and you now know a lot about keeping it that way. You might say you have a few paternal tricks of the trade up your muscular sleeve when it comes to toddler-bedtime.

For example, you know how to be at your boring best. You know how to time the snack perfectly, with tummy-filling ingredients that satisfy but don't stimulate. You know to keep the lights low. You know where the special blankie is—at all times—and how to tuck it in just right. You know to keep the water-filled sippy cup close at hand so you don't have to leave the room and fetch. You know how to wish inanimate objects "sweet dreams" within a thirty-yard radius.

But there's just no way you can know everything about toddler-bedtime even if you live to be a happy grandpappy of 103. Here, father-friend, are a few reasons why.

YOU KNOW   it's 11:45 p.m., your 18-month-old is screaming—again—and you have to get up at 6:30 a.m. to get him ready for day care and catch the bus to work

YOU DON'T KNOW   how much longer you can keep your bloodshot eyes open even if he can't close his

YOU KNOW   the audio monitor is a fiendish device and you'd like to smash it into a million pieces every time your daughter howls

YOU DON'T KNOW   why you are using the audio monitor since anyone with normal ears could hear her from anywhere in your zip code

[144]

YOU KNOW   no matter what time it is in the wee hours of the morning, neither you nor your toddler should turn to the bottle for relief from this bedtime insanity

YOU DON'T KNOW   how much longer the *Jack Daniel's* and *Carnation* can stay locked up in their respective cabinets

YOU KNOW   you could grab a blanket and take a nap on the floor under the crib until your daughter goes to sleep, even though all the toddler guides say it's a No-No

YOU DON'T KNOW   whether the cat will share the space with you

YOU KNOW   between outbursts, you might sit your sobbing son in your lap and carefully explain to him why sleep is important so that he can grow up healthy and strong, and especially so that he might have a good day tomorrow

YOU DON'T KNOW   why anyone would think of such a stupid idea

YOU KNOW   you will have terrible guilt feelings in the morning if you decide—for the first time—to let your toddler cry herself to sleep tonight

YOU DON'T KNOW   if your toddler will cry herself to sleep or just keep crying

YOU KNOW   you made a terrible mistake when, earlier in the day, you sent your toddler to time-out in his crib simply for pulling the dog's tail. Now it's time for nite-nite and your little man is standing, gripping the bars of the crib like a blubbering criminal on death row

YOU DON'T KNOW   why you got carried away with punishment, capital or otherwise. After your toddler shared his ice cream with him, the dog refused to press charges

YOU KNOW   you've got major trouble when your three-year-old's bawling ignites the baby in the next room, producing stereophonic pandemonium

YOU DON'T KNOW   which hell-pit to walk into first

YOU KNOW   you've worked hard to become the most boring person on the planet. You know because your incredibly dull personality and monotonous routine have your two-year-old sawing logs in less than five minutes

YOU DON'T KNOW   recently, why your workmates seem to fall asleep in their cubicles when they see you coming

YOU KNOW   your daughter pops up like a jack-in-the-box the minute you close her bedroom door

YOU DON'T KNOW   if attaching bungee cords to her crib rails and stretching them tight horizontally, six inches above her mattress would do any good

YOU KNOW   it was a mistake to flip the light switch on a few minutes ago when you walked in to comfort your weeping son. You just forgot, that's all

[146]

YOU DON'T KNOW   why your son never wakes up when your inconsiderate neighbor from across the street comes home and backs into his driveway shining high-beams into your son's window. But your glad

YOU KNOW   Mommy would be here helping you through this sleeptime nightmare if she could, but she had to spend the night at your mother-in-law's to help her decorate her living room for the holidays

YOU DON'T KNOW   when the decorating will be done; you're just glad your mother-in-law's decorating at *her* house for a change

YOU KNOW   narcolepsy is a serious health problem, but could your toddler give it a temporary try for the next year or two?

⌐   ⌐   ⌐   ⌐   ⌐

Lullaby Encore: Standing Room Only

Naptimes Can Be Nightmares Too

Most of the stuff you've learned (and unlearned) about toddler-bedtimes can be applied to naptimes too. But discerning dads on top of their toddler game know there can be subtle differences as well.

Take the customized toddler-daddy bedtime routine. *Please. Take it. Treat it like leftover toddler-dinner scraps, throw it in a garbage disposal, grind it up and send it to the sewer.* No. No. Just kidding. Have faith in your routine, even if it backfires on you some evenings. The point is, if you have faith in your trusty routine, you can transfer many of its nighttime elements to daytime nap duty.

Keep a quiet attitude for 20 minutes or so prior to nappy. Start shushing out the world (and the daytime light). If it's afternoon, a filled up tummy right after lunch makes for prime napping time. Morning? Pack a snack into the old pie hole—but better avoid pies, rich cookies and cake. Yep. Too much sugar makes for jumpy toddler neurons.

The main trouble with naps (other than the fact that you could use a nap more than your toddler) is that you have to coordinate them chronologically with bedtime. Late afternoon nappies, for example, turn nite-nite into a nightmarish non-happening. Plus, young toddlers tend to need two naps. But three- to four-year-olds won't stand for twin putting-downs, so don't bother.

Ideally, along about 36-months, you're looking for a predictable toddler-schedule that includes a reasonable waking hour (not too pre-dawnish), an early afternoon nap (say, 1-1/2 to 2-1/2 hours), and keeping your fingers and toes crossed, capped off with the saving grace of all toddler households—*the magical early bedtime.*

Now, you might truly be the most dedicated, dependable, determined daddy ever to stroll down your neighborhood sidewalk with toddler-care medals dangling all over the breast pocket of your apron. But coordinating number of naps + nap duration + regular bedtime + ideal morning wake-up ÷ routines for all of the above isn't easy to finesse.

If you're a dad who can do it precisely with perfect regularity day after day, week after week...then you're either a cow farmer who's had years of experience doing double-shifts in the milking parlor, a premier juggler for *Cirque du Soleil,* or a mathematical genius.

If not...if you're more like the rest of us poor souls sloughing our way through a steady sewer-stream of toddler-care setbacks, you can still take heart. You can still be a happy nappy pappy. You can still be a beddy-bye champ, not a loser-chump.

One way is to read the following list of toddler sleep-care insights. Taken from a research paper documenting a unique clinical study of toddler insomniacs, these observations certainly hit home. You might discover one or two that speak directly to you. You might find two or three that hit the nail on the head. If not, you can continue to hit yourself over the head as you and your toddler battle over sleep, night and day.

[150]

Little Known Facts
about Toddler Insomniacs

——After interrogation, toddlers known as "midnight ram-
blers" admit the reason why they ramble is because they can't
sleep, so they don't want adults in the house to sleep either

——North American "urban" toddlers record naptimes averaging 2.1 hours. North American "rural" toddlers record naptimes averaging 1.7 hours. The difference? Toddlers on the
farm report daily chores keep their napping to a minimum

——The word "nap" is not a word in many cultures outside
North America

——The ranking president of the European Toddler Union
(*ETU*) was recently re-elected on a campaign advocating late-
night toddies, early-morning cappuccinos and midday dessert
smorgasbords for toddlers worldwide

——27.6 is the average number of consecutive days recorded
by the average toddler continuing to scream for his milk ba-
ba after being successfully weaned from nite-nite feeding

——4.6 is the average number of attempts the average toddler will make to jump out of his crib and find his own nite-
nite bottle; Multiplied by 6 if he succeeds

——7% of interviewed toddlers indicate they are fearful of
soothing, warm baths prior to bedtime. 100% of these are guar-
anteed not to become Olympic Gold Medal swimmers

——78 is the record-holding number of stuffed animals stuffed into an individual toddler's crib as part of the bedtime ritual. Unfortunately, her parents have not been able to locate said toddler since the record was established

——Among multiple-choice answers, toddler interviewees selected, top to bottom: (a) depressing, (b) infantile, (c) laughable, and (d) worthwhile to describe parents' use of "gold-star" charts as tools to record/reward sleeptime achievements

——89% of sampled toddlers said "No Comment" when asked to comment on their favorite father-lullaby

——Number one late-night television show for toddler night owls? Reruns of *Rugrats*. Number two? *Seinfeld*.

——Number one asked-for comfort object in the crib for toddler nite-nite? *Mommy*. Number two? *Mommy*.

Chapter eight

Toilet Training Builds a Pant-Load of Trust

Grab your noseplugs and join the party.
Peeing and pooping in the potty is a great experience
for the whole family!

—inspiration from a popular toddler-care book

⌐   ⌐   ⌐   ⌐   ⌐   ⌐   ⌐

As men, we understand the complexities of life on a basic, instinctive level. We can thank our caveman heritage. Thousands of years later, evolution has taken its toll, but we still have good instincts. Women may have taken over the intellectual reins to some extent, especially in child-rearing, but we masculine types still have a knack for operating on a truly simplistic level when we need to. We still recognize a fundamental truth when we see it. We know sex is great in the morning. We know sinking a 35-foot putt on the 18th hole is almost as good. We understand that fishing, hiking, baseball, Chinese checkers and reading are better than shopping.

In sports, males recognize the waste that goes on off the field, the overpaid professionals leading adolescent lives, the ridiculous salaries and inflated ticket prices...but we still love a day at the ballpark. The roar of the crowd, the hot dogs, the beer. We see through the crap and still appreciate seeing great players make great plays under pressure.

That's how we know there is absolutely nothing great about seeing pee-pee and poo-poo. Neither one is good to smell or touch. Further, neither one is good to listen to being done.

Taking out the garbage is better. Smearing your hand over a grease-covered V8 valve cover is better. Changing a tire on the side of the freeway and stripping your lug nuts is better. Even packed in a subway with your nose stuck in a fitness instructor's smelly armpit is a better experience than fondling pee-pee and poo-poo.

I hate going to the dentist, but it's better. Attending two-hour PTA meetings? Better. Traveling cross-country in a compact car with your wife, toddler and mother-in-law? Better. Going to the proctologist? Maybe.

And unlike a professional athlete, the fact is you don't have to have a whiff of talent to be fantastic at pee-peeing and poo-pooing.

All this said, as a father, I admit that close encounters with another human's urine and feces wouldn't be sooooo bad if you could just take a look and say, "Yippee! What a great job! Now clean yourself up and let's get going."

Because, gentlemen, I'm afraid to tell you that it's not quite that easy.

The problem with the advice at the beginning of the chapter about *peeing and pooping in the potty being a great experience*...is that this lovely waste matter—liquid or solid, captured and contained or unrestrained and roaming freely—doesn't end up in the potty FOR A LONG, LONG PERIOD OF TIME.

That's right. They don't call it training for nothing. And that's the real scoop on poop.

In truth when you're in the midst of human waste training, it will seem like years—no, more like an eternity—before your eager-to-please student achieves success. Simply put, that means the stuff could end up *anywhere*.

So slip into your (camouflage) jumpsuit, strap on your pooper scooper, clip on your badge, grab your nose clips and get ready to lead the troops around the perimeter of your dwelling. Be sure to inspect behind doors, in corners and closets. Check the kitty litter box and the aquarium for unauthorized use. That's right, mister. Till you receive further orders, you're on...

<u>permanent poop patrol</u>.

The Most Incredible Invention of the Century

Yes, finding piles here and there, collecting the mess, mopping floors, wiping hineys, and scrubbing soiled panties—these are all part of your new doo-doo duties. After some time, you might find yourself questioning your role. You might start thinking about working on the FRONT END of the problem instead of the BACK END.

It's natural. You're a leader at heart; you want to get more involved. You want to create a solution, other than an ammonia-based cleaning one. You want to be the first true genius of the new century. You want everyone to know you as THE MAN who invented...

overnight toilet training

That's cool. May I be the first to wish you God speed and dazzling good luck. Because if you succeed in inventing overnight toilet training, even without a marketing budget, you would be the richest man alive in less than six months.

And it wouldn't matter whether your genius idea is linked to pills, straps, wine corks, cough medicine, potty seat magnets, pulleys, far eastern chants, hypnotism, meditation or medication...your brilliant *Overnight Potty Training for Toddlers Scheme* would cure all of your parenting problems and make you a billionaire without a care.

[156]

Of course you do need to be made aware that however extraordinary your concept is, you are most assuredly not the first person who has attempted it.

Anthropology studies prove fathers far back in the prehistoric mists worked tirelessly on toddler-related potty inventions. Before tasting de-feat (and giving in to da-stink) each believed he would uncover a way to deliver us from evil. Fresh from the discovery of fire, our ancestor-dads pushed hard for a second world-class breakthrough: a sure-fire way to quickly pry the poop from the (animal-skin) pants and deliver it to the potty.

After a rocky start the guy who later invented the wheel gave up on constructing a tot-size, volcanic-action cave toilet. Instead, he decided to invent a faster way of getting away from the stench. Plato, Alexander the Great and Caesar all worked on their inventions, too. Some say Caesar was getting close, but he got stabbed by a group of impatient fathers who couldn't wait for THE PLAN.

Now here we are in the early years of a new century, and the RAPID POOP PLAN is still an elusive vision. But it's hard to let go. No dad wants to surrender the dream. Yet, dear comrade-dad, the truth is overnight potty success will *always* be an unfulfilled fantasy. The other fact we have to face is that it's just not healthy walking around with doo-doo on your mind all the time. In the end, when you think about it, it's really a crappy idea. So do your very best to wipe it out of your thought patterns.

My best advice is to take a natural approach to one of life's natural functions. Don't invent. Don't intervene. Don't expect too much. Don't inspect too much.

In other words,

Don't Be a Party Pooper to Your Potty Pooper

If you stick your nose in where it doesn't belong—too close to your toddler's business—you might discover your two-year-old is suddenly frozen in time, with nothing but poo-poo on his mind, and an empty potty under his behind. Keep pressuring for progress and before you know it you'll have a constipation crisis on your hands. Your poor toddler could become

Too Popped to Poop

Don't let this happen to the two of you. Guard against over-eager time tables. Keep rewards (and bribes) to a minimum. Restrict your use of wipe-free tracking charts and personal computers to record progress. Especially leave digital cameras out of the picture. In other words, don't get too passionate about this poop thing. As Dad, you've got to be at your cool, calm, masculine best. You can't afford to get your poopmeter in an uproar.

Put all those misguided thoughts of glory behind you. If you feel you have to take a crack at being a potty chair hero, be sure you don't let the bottom fall out of your commitment to the impromptu poo-poo. Don't risk getting in over your head. Most of all, if you want natural results, you need to take a low-profile, natural approach.

Going with The Flow

Potty training can still be a lot of hard work even if you're a dad with a relaxed attitude. But who wants to make this grueling event more difficult and complicated than it needs to be? I mean, it's the purest form of grunt work you're ever likely to encounter. So let's start with the basics.

First off, you have to buy a potty and put it in the bathroom. Your wife will assume you know this already, so don't tell her if you didn't. If you're like me, maybe you thought your toddlerette could start training on the big people's toilet. A few do. But to most toddlers, that big white toilet is about the size of a small pond. It's harder to grip and grunt so high up. And it's too far down to the water as well. In fact, your child might rate perching on the big people's commode about as much fun as squatting over the top of a deep well. The idea of a scary, splashy explosion isn't exactly what the two of you want to think about when it's potty time.

Your wife will probably choose a cute little potty with bunnies on it. Don't question the design. Bunnies and BM's go together great. The cuter it is, the longer you can sit there letting your mind wander, wondering, *who designs these things, anyway?* Anything to help the time pass more quickly.

[159]

Along with its mandatory cute design, the potty may hold a couple of other convenient, clever features that you will notice with your keen papa vision and virile powers of perception. See the little plastic bowl under the seat? It slides out. Isn't that convenient? See the little "deflector" hump at the front of the seat? That's for "stream of consciousness" thinking that sometimes takes place when your son's busy concentrating on his B.M. Isn't that clever?

If only the little deflector had a self-cleaning feature. If only the bowl would fly out of the potty, scrub itself off and return without your assistance. If only you could hook up a garden hose to that little hiney.

Oh, well. At least you've chosen the right potty and it's in the right bathroom (any one but yours), and ready for his use anytime he is moved to use it. Now all you have to do is wait till he displays signs of readiness.

Pop's Top Ten
Toddler Poop & Pee Signs

Get Ready...Get Set...Go!

TEN   He walks in on you while you're using the potty and says casually, "What's up, Pop?"—the first time he's ever strung together three words in his life

NINE   You notice your son standing in the middle of the sunroom, peeing freely as usual, the flow leaking through the gather of his training pants and cascading into his socks. But for the very first time—he notices too

EIGHT   Your son waddles into the garage holding his neatly taped, loaded diaper in one hand, opens up the garbage can lid and tosses the contents in

SEVEN   The next day your son waddles over to the litter box in the garage and says, "Go pee-pee, kee-kee," whereupon he tosses the kitty in

SIX   In an historic first, the young lad wakes up from his afternoon nap with a perfectly dry Huggies

FIVE   After attending a poop party and watching his older cousin deliver a big B.M., he asks where's his own potty. Mommy tells him it's sitting next to the bathtub just like it has been for the past four months

FOUR   One day, diaper-clad, he leaps out from his hidden poo corner and repeatedly shouts, "POOPS SMELL! POOPS SMELL!" You sigh at the sky and say, "Bingo!"

THREE   Sonny has soiled 36 disposable training pants in five days, but insists on wearing them instead of diapers

TWO   Daily, he poops in his diaper at 10:00, 2:00 and 4:00—as regular as an old-fashioned bottle of Dr. Pepper

ONE   After saying "No!" 1,292 times in a row to the question, "Would you like to go potty now?"...your son stuns you by throwing down his toys, smiling, and saying, "Yes."

TWO THUMBS UP!
Praising the Pooper till Your Potty Runneth Over

As a veteran poop-meister on patrol, one of your finest contributions can be keeping the poop experience positive. Growing up to be the tough-minded, masculine patriarch you are, you've faced life's challenges, fought your way through the rigors of education and found a productive spot in our 21st century workforce. Along the way you learned that disappointments happen. You make a bad grade. You get passed over for a promotion. You pass on the BMW and buy the Dodge Caravan.

Worst of all, every year, your trip to Europe gets postponed and you settle for a week at your in-law's in Ohio.

Yet you learn to grit your teeth and march on, concentrating on making babies, and afterward, being the best dad you can be. It's the same with your sweet toddler's toilet learning. There will be setbacks. Bad days. Worse days. Days when you step forward one and step back three. Still, life-sculpted and wiser by the minute, you maintain a mommy-like serenity.

As the old saying goes, that means you approach all facets of potty-pooping by *accentuating the positive.*

You anticipate the coming of a B.M. with ooohhs and aaahhhhs and hushed appreciation during the process. Upon deliverance, you praise the specimen as if it were an unrivaled

[162]

work of art, an original sculpture of unprecedented beauty. That doesn't necessarily mean you want to capture it, preserve it and immortalize it under glass on top of your mantel. Just admire the stool as much as possible, up to your up-chuck limit. Try not to grimace, groan or let your eyes water.

If you have to attach a clothespin to your nose and breathe through your mouth, tell your toddler, "Daddy has a cold. It's nothing personal."

During the hiney-wiping phase, be precise, use an oversized, thick wipe and never let your hand slip. Since your child's backside will be facing you at this point, it's permissible to make a face, bare your teeth and stick out your tongue in disgust. But don't make any negative sounds or comments such as, "YOWZA, THIS IS ONE NASTY BUTT!" And remember...don't let your hand slip.

After wiping clean, pulling up the training pants and turning her around, you can smile and sing, "You're a clean machine, Geraldine! Clap your hands and slap your jeans. You don't wear a diaper 'cause you're a Potty Queen!"

Then, two days later, you might find yourself singing the training-pants blues. Uncle Bud came to visit and she pooped on his shoes. You forgot to haul her into the bathroom before church and Geraldine went number two in the pew. They hid the bathroom so well in the department store that you gave up in Lingerie and pee-peed on the spot. Okay?

Whatever setbacks you encounter in your journey from stinky Diaper Mountain to the pure, wind-swept gates of

Potty Paradise, you need to demonstrate a saintly measure of paternal patience. Sure, there are yellow splashes on your Oriental rugs. Yes, the fragrance of Pine-Sol fills your living room. Right, the back seat of your sedan smells like a hog farm.

Just the same you can believe your daughter will get the potty-protocol down. She'll be peeing and pooping in porcelain, before long, with the best of them. Stay positive. And don't fret. You won't have to sit in the audience of her high school graduation worrying about the diaper bulges under her robe as she reaches for the diploma.

Promise.

The Full Load Pappy-Poopy Probe

Are you a true *Super Poop-Man*? How do you rank when things get truly rank? When the commode stops up and overflows from a mountainous load of stool-packed cloth training pants. When the foul odor makes you alter the pleasant French *eau de toilette* to *Oh! The Toilet!* When mounds of what you thought (at first glance) was chunky peanut butter smeared along the hallway baseboard turn out to be something slightly darker and less pleasant to the touch.

Are you mommy-enough to take decisive action when the you-know-what hits the fan during your toddler's upcoming weekend poopathon? Do you have the maternal know-how when the bottom falls out of your no-hassle, Saturday afternoon poop plan? Are you armed with the latest techniques all the female troops employ on poop patrol? Can you name every popular brand of cleanser you'll need the next time you're ankle-deep in diarrhea?

Whether you answered yes or no to the preceding questions, it's time to step up to the potty and test your poop wits. You need to know exactly how you compare in all things toddler-derriére. Will you stand or fold the next time your face-to-face with a royal flush? In the midst of a public pooping crisis, how does your decision-making stack up against your papa peers?

In the upcoming exam, you'll have every chance to demonstrate your superior potty intellect. For the first time ever in a Clearing Skies Press multiple choice test, you will have *two bonus questions* in order to boost your score.

It's your chance to climb up from the dung heap of toddler-care mediocrity and bowl your wife over with your Grade A poop knowledge. Once and for all, when she sees your test score, you'll prove to her how much crap you *really* have on your mind.

Even if you're not a regular fan of human feces, you'll find this quiz quite a challenge. But don't be a poop and try to peek at the answers. Ever since cub scouts, you've known that honesty's the best policy. So cover each answer with your hand or a bookmark, then make an intelligent choice without cheating.

Best of luck getting a *head* start on your competitors. It's always better to be *johnny* on the spot than to *stall* around. So take a seat, get comfortable, and *go* already.

START OF TEST
(please, no peeking)

Question:

Your sweet 23-month-old daughter, sitting behind you in the grocery cart, takes off her soiled diaper and throws it on top of the ice cream cartons in the frozen food section. Should you?

> (a) Say, "That's a sh_tty thing to do!"
> (b) Say, "Beverly, is that a hint that you'd like chocolate instead of vanilla?"
> (c) Say, "Bev, sit your naked butt back down in the cart!"
> (d) Place the inflatable toilet seat you carried in your day pack over the grocery cart seat, let her limbs dangle through the leg holes and say, "Go, Baby, Go!"

The answer is
(b). While (a) is a natural response, it's profane and solves nothing...unworthy of a talented toilet trainer like you. You could use (c) to back up (a), but your job's to teach Beverly about the potty, and this command has no instructional value. Nice try with (d), but it's like striking out on a high fastball. You're way late, baby. With (b) you're making a casual mental note about Beverly's signs of readiness for potty learning, plus you're gaining on tomorrow's lunch menu—a bonus.

Question:

Your semi-trained son is prancing around the kitchen bare-chested, looking like an alien with a colander on his head and a load of poop jiggling in his training pants. Should you?

(a) Scream, "You STINK as an entertainer!"

(b) Tell him there is positively no exotic dancing allowed in your community, by order of the city council

(c) Tuck a dollar in his pants and applaud his showmanship

(d) Hand him wipes and a fresh pair of undies, commenting, "I like the inter-galactic look, but everyone on this planet uses the potty. Once you finish cleaning up, you'll understand why."

The answer is
(d). Once again, (a) is honest, but it's negative and could talk your son out of a rewarding stage career. Why do it? (b) is over his head while (c) may encourage his pursuit of an unsavory stage career. (d) is a pure power-flush, teaching fitting-in, self-reliance and work ethic, all rolled into one.

Question:

In front of a room full of visiting relatives, your sonny-buck saunters over, pulls down his training pants and pees on the ficus tree. Should you?

(a) Applaud him for noticing the parched houseplant

(b) Comment on the excellent power of his stream

(c) Pass around the pitcher of lemonade, asking politely "Would you care for a refill?"

(d) Brag to the crowd, "Ain't he a natural? Wait till you see him do Number Two!"

The answer is
(c). You know Mommy struggles to keep her favorite house-plants alive, so (a) is nice, except there's way too much acidity in urine for the good of the plant. Sorry. (b) indicates a touch of envy considering your aging prostate—better keep it to your-self. (c) is polite and glosses over the incident, a good choice. But if your guests look suspiciously at the pitcher's contents, you might have to look for another solution. (d) is crude and might scare your company, plus remember, bragging is only permitted as potty praise between you and your son.

Question:

You watch amused as your sweet toddlerette follows the boxer into the master bathroom—imitating him—then you watch horrified as she pushes him out of the way and starts to lap from the toilet doggy-style. Should you?

(a) Offer her a swim mask and snorkel
(b) Say, "Just a minute, young lady. You know we don't bob for apples until Halloween."
(c) Slap the boxer on the butt, then tell him he's a wimp for giving up his turf to the toddler
(d) Re-install the toilet lid latch which you removed just two days ago for toddler toilet training

The answer is
(b). Gotcha! If you're like me, you're proud of being a man with a logical brain. So you selected (d). Well, let this be a les-son to you. There's very little logic involved with toddlers and parenting. (a)? Just a tad irresponsible, don't you think? Answer

(c) accomplishes nothing. Give your boxer some credit. Even with bobbed ears and tail, he knows how much it hurts when a mad toddler yanks on them. Here's the poop-scoop on (d)... you can't risk latches on toilet lids 'cause there's no time to spare—when the toddler's gotta go, she's gotta go. Not only does (b) stop her; it makes her laugh and preserves the traditions of an important holiday.

Question:

Tragically, rushing to pull his pants down and sit him on the potty, you tip your son over on his elbows, butt pointed in the air, and he then sprays you in the face with poop. Should you?

> (a) Shriek hysterically, "Chunky mudpies—me want more!"
> (b) Pass out
> (c) Wail out the window, "Somebody call the Red Cross!"
> (d) Stick your head in the big toilet and flush, repeatedly

The answer is
(d). Well, if you missed this one, you deserve your fate in the cruel rating system waiting for you at the end of the test. They don't get any easier. What's up with (a)? There's a response that could only be called *scary*. (b) means total abandonment of your faculties and fatherly duties—no dice. (c) is the wrong organization. You need the International Plumbers Union, IPU for short. (d) Ah, yes. Immediate action that's instinctive, masculine and creative. The perfect rapid-fire solution to a rapid-fire problem!

Question:

Frozen like a statue on top of her toy chest, your daughter grunts loudly as you watch her fill her drawers. Noticing you, she says sternly, "Don't look, Da-Da. Don't look!" Should you?

> (a) Leap on the box beside her, barking, "I'm the original *Poop-Meister*, who do you think you're toying with?"
> (b) Reply, "Whatever you say, you crazy poo-poo-in-the-pants kid."
> (c) Reply, "But if I can't look, can I at least smell?"
> (d) Bring in a kitchen bowl and soup ladle, announcing, "Okay, gal—time for lunch! Let's scoop & serve those chocolate mashed potatoes you keep requesting."

The answer is

(a). Okay, this type of setback is tough to take, I know. But you have to stay strong. (b) is pure capitulation, a sad choice. (c) borders on bizarre, good for masochists, maybe. (d) blends sickening and bizarre, a disgusting idea at best. (a) projects a confident, uniquely paternal response. Plus, you're applying your super-hero tendencies to potty-training. Excellent!

Question:

Your 42-month-old darling son is the last diaper-wearer left in his day care class. One weekend your Aunt Bernice is visiting the two of you. Suddenly, she pinches her nose and exclaims, "Peeeeeee-Youuuuuuu. Don't tell me you still let this kid crap in his pants!" What should you do?

(a) Tell Auntie, "That's about enough of your bullcrap."

(b) Tell Auntie, "If you got a brilliant idea from the ancient annals of toddler-anal training, let me know."

(c) Say, "Quit your complaining and get some room fragrance over here—can't you see we're suffocating?"

(d) Walk out the front door, remarking, "Well, he's your grand nephew, Bernie—this is your big chance to put your poop prescription where your know-it-all mouth is."

The answer is

(c). If you can steel yourself and avoid yielding to answer (d) (a just and terrible temptation), then your choices are clear-cut. (a) is insulting to an aunt you've always regarded with affection; (b) takes (a)'s needless insult a step further. That leaves (c), not a perfect choice, but no one ever said poopy-training is perfect (or even bearable, as opposed to bare-able).

Question:

You're in your neighborhood public library holding your toddler's hand, patiently waiting in line to check out books. You smell something, look down and see a dark glob sliding down your daughter's ankle, engulfing the top of her tennis shoe. Should you?

(a) Pick her up and fly to the rest room

(b) Forget the rest room; pull the fire alarm instead

(c) Stick to your plan and calmly check out your books

(d) Stick the glob under the bottom of her shoe and complain bitterly to the librarian, "Someone *must* enforce the no-dog policy in here."

The answer is
Again, (c). Another easy one—hope you made it count. Imagine legs dangling, slashing through the narrow stacks in (a), splattering the fiction section with feces—not a real-world option. (b) calls for violating the law and adding panic to the poop, not a good mix. Unless you can whip out a super-size wipe and practice sleight-of-hand like a magician, nobody's buying (d). You might find (c) boring at first glance, but it's sneaky-smart and may get you to the head of the line quickly once the poop-news starts spreading and people start dropping out of line like flies.

BONUS QUESTIONS

Congratulations! You've earned a great big B.M.-bonus by straining hard, hanging in there, and squeezing out a correct answer or two. Even if you suffered from severe mental blockage or impacted brain syndrome and couldn't fill the answer bowl with *anything*, you now get a second chance: Two special bonus questions, never before available on a "Pop" quiz, poop-absorbed or not.

Now you can start fresh and wipe the slate clean, so to speak, by answering two in a row right. At this point, you may not end up high on the Pappy-Poopy throne, but perhaps you can avoid sitting on the lowest form of stool with a Zero-Maggot rating.

Time to really dig in to the subject matter...

Bonus Question #1:

After months of unsuccessful toileting, you and your toddler walk hand-in-hand out back of your great-uncle Elmer's farmhouse. You spy the old outhouse with the half-moon cutout and suddenly have a brilliant thought. What's the big idea?

> (a) A unique 21st century toddler-potty solution using 19th century facilities
> (b) Spiders, snakes, corncobs, catalogs and cobwebs— special friends and a special atmosphere for a special, down-home poop party
> (c) Permanently redefining the word "stench" in your toddler-potty vocabulary
> (d) Making your son understand, once and for all, that it's a rotten idea to hate his potty—it isn't half as bad as he thought

The answer is
(d). Let him swivel the wooden door latch and poke his head inside one time. He'll get the message! On the other hand, (a), you can't really *use* the outhouse—your wife would kill you. (Even though *he* was potty-trained there, Uncle Elmer doesn't even use the outhouse anymore unless Aunt Maggie's using the indoor plumbing. Plus, he orders everything on the Internet these days and hasn't owned a Sears catalog for years.) No way for (b), if Mommy won't accept (a). Answer (c) might wield psychological power as a lead-in for (d), but you still wind up with (d), regardless.

Uncle Elmer's Special Potty

Bonus Question #2:

On Mommy's orders, after months of frustration and failure, you put the potty on the lawn and let your 37-month-old sweetie have a fun afternoon frolicking buck-naked in your fenced backyard. Around 4:00 p.m. your beagle heists his leg and pees on a tree, prompting your daughter to plop down on her potty and do the same. At this moment, your widow-neighbor Mrs. Pearson peeks over the fence and gasps. Should you?

> (a) Say, cordially, "Hi, there, neighbor. It's clothing-optional on this side of the fence—care to join us?"
> (b) Say, firmly, "This potty-party is invitation-only. Butt out, you old goat!"
> (c) Say, sarcastically, "Hey, Peeping-Tom Pearson—buy a ticket and stick around. The dog and I go together in Act II."
> (d) Ignore Mrs. Pearson and rave to the world, "Yiiiiiiiiiiiii-*pee*...sweet deliverance!"

Again, (d). Another free kick and empty net for you gentlemen to take advantage of..."Pop" quiz scoring has never been easier. With any luck, a correct response here will lift you off the cow pie pile. Let's review the choices. (a)? Toss this answer quick unless you want to see your elderly neighbor hopping around nude on your lawn. (b) Turns a gracious invitation into a hostile non-invitation. For what? With a sense of showmanship, you could pretend you're P.T. Barnum and let it all hang out by choosing (c)—but Pearson might call the police, spoiling your performance. (d) indicates total devotion to the potty experience, and remember, you get to proudly show your wife the contents afterward. Ain't life beautiful?

The Full Load
Pappy-Poopy Probe
Official Score and Occupation

You may not be the world's greatest Poo-Poo Guru, or the premier commander of Operation Pee-Pee-in-the-Potty, but you probably still have strong feelings about toilet training. Everyone seems to. Plus, being male, liberal or conservative, new-age or old-fashioned, you still sport a competitive spirit. That's why, standing eye-to-eye opposite your comrade dads, potty-to-potty in a test of wills, you want to do well. At minimum you want to achieve a socially acceptable ranking. Preferably, a poopy-occupation with more prestige than the toddler-father across the street who brags incessantly about how incredibly smart he and his kids are.

You know your neighbor's fudging when he says, every time he's in charge, his two-year-old craps in the big people's toilet like a lumberjack with an enema. And the results are so artistic, the braggart dad has taken to calling his son, Van *Gogh*. Van Gogh this, Van Gogh that. Up and down the sidewalk.

You want to post a more lofty score than a guy like that, but you figure the jackass is probably cheating anyway. If his wife supervised the test-taking, the man would be slinking around trying to shake off the stigma of *Sewer Rat*. Instead, he struts around talking about crushing the Poopy-Probe and achieving the status of *Ace Plumber*.

[176]

If you know a neighbor like this, remember one thing. Real life is the true test and how you perform one-on-one with your toddler is what really counts. As a father, imperfect as you may be, you will always give the toddler-toilet your best shot. You know too that multiple choice tests are as flawed as you.

Even so, the time has come to chart your answers, tally the score and look for your certified rating below. With any luck, in another decade or so, you'll be able to eliminate all fears of toilet training and feel good about waste matters again.

Score ten points for each correct answer and assign yourself a lifelong occupational status.

Score	Official Poop Occupation
0	Maggot
10	Cow Pie
20	Sewer Rat
30	Bathroom Attendant
40	Outhouse Technician
50	Port-a-John Apprentice
60	Cesspool Inspector
70	Janitor
80	Ex-Lax® Executive
90	Ty-D-Bol® Inventor
100	*ACE PLUMBER*

Chapter nine

Toddlers Are Like Teens, Only Smaller

*...they will turn and bite
the hand that fed them*

—Edmund Burke

⌐ ⌐ ⌐ ⌐ ⌐ ⌐ ⌐

Special Note:

In a universal tribute to both toddlers and teens, children of every culture, ages two to four and 13 to 18, this chapter will be short. Just like their attention spans.

Personally, after raising one of each gender from tender infant-hood to traumatic adolescent-hood, I've spent a lot of time looking under the hood, and I can assure you that your offspring are amazingly complex. Quicker and more complicated and much more dangerous than a Formula One racing car running on jet fuel. In other words, from Baby forward, you better have quick wits and fast reflexes if you want to keep up with them.

Yet the only thing nearly as fast as kids changing is how quickly they manage to change you.

Simple modifications... lighthearted adjustments... minor reversals... would not the world be sweet if gentle alterations were the sum of our children's impact. But Baby is just the beginning.

With Infants come changes.
With Toddlers come calamities.
With Teens come cataclysms.

It's a progression. Along with the miracle and joy of Baby, you wake bewildered in the middle of the night—those nights when Baby doesn't wake you first, that is—asking aloud, *could someone please tell me what's going on here?*

Then, amazingly, by the time your first-born has hit the throes of toddlerhood, you're getting accustomed to a kid-dominated planet. You've practically lost touch with that former world you used to lounge in...that cheerful, childless, thrill-seeking amusement park...the kid-free kingdom of pleasure you sipped from on a whim.

[180]

Now, instead of flirting all day in the house of mirrors and hitting roller-coaster peaks in the tunnel of love, you and your wife are trapped in a freaky sideshow world of dwarf-like creatures, little contortionists who roller-coaster wildly around your living room, crashing into objects (and each other) like bumper cars gone berserk.

Instead of a quiet love-nest made for a romantic couple with leisure time to burn, your home is now a crazy spook-house with screams and cries echoing off the walls, unworldly smells infusing the woodwork, and toddler-care demands so thick there is no time for adult bowel movements, let alone parental romance.

Your home, your life, your soul has been taken over by your toddler.

Being the intelligent male progenitor of the clan, you adjust. Your wife, wise and tolerant, helps you adjust. Nevertheless, you would still like to pose a parental-type question of the paternal variety. Such as, when will you again regain control over your existence? Or, when will this bizarre, three-ring circus shut down so you can shovel the sawdust off the floor and live like normal human beings again?

Well, father-brother, like most things in life—like everything to do with toddlers and teens—your question brings GOOD NEWS and BAD NEWS.

⌐   ⌐   ⌐   ⌐   ⌐

THE GOOD NEWS   your toddler is learning to talk, so that before you know it, he will be able to express himself so articulately that you will actually enjoy speaking with him

THE BAD NEWS   when he becomes a teenager, he will give up voluntary conversation altogether

THE GOOD NEWS   your toddlerette still likes to give you hugs, even though she's growing up

THE BAD NEWS   your teen will like to give you hugs, if you have your credit card handy when she asks

THE GOOD NEWS   your little boy eats like a horse, though occasionally not the best foods, and he's growing like a weed, now inching up the chart on his bedroom wall

THE BAD NEWS   your teen will eat like a herd of wild horses, though rarely anything healthy, and he'll still be growing like a weed, soon towering over his mother and blocking the sun from your office window

THE GOOD NEWS   your toddler sweetheart knows how to say "please" and "thank you" and she even listens to you (sometimes) when you explain about the importance of manners and being considerate to others

THE BAD NEWS   your adolescent daughter uses good manners (you've been told) everywhere but home where she's selfish, rude and militant about her undisputed status as *The Center of the Universe*

[182]

THE GOOD NEWS   Toddler Tom, the apple of your eye, happily says, "Wead..." "Dwaw..." and "Pway Ball..." when you ask him what he did during his school day

THE BAD NEWS   Teenage Tom, still the apple of your eye, will grumble "Not much..." "Stuff..." and "Nothing..." when you ask him what he did during his school day

THE GOOD NEWS   every night when you get home from work, your little girl sits on your knee and talks to you about tea parties, doll dresses and puppy dog tails

THE BAD NEWS   every night when you get home from work, your teenage lass will sit on the Internet for hours *instant messaging* her friends about weekend parties, clothes to buy and pubescent boy tales

THE GOOD NEWS   your toddy boy loves the quiet time of an animated film on television, though not to the point of falling asleep like he used to when he was a baby

THE BAD NEWS   your teenage sloth-lad will love to sit in front of the tube for days on end watching *Comedy Central* until his eyeballs fall out and he turns comatose

THE GOOD NEWS   your toddler darling is learning to control her emotions, notably in public places, where tantrum incidents are becoming less and less frequent

THE BAD NEWS   your teen daughter will learn to control your emotions, notably in public places like shopping malls, where your wallet will become less and less filled

[183]

THE GOOD NEWS   Watch Attentive Junior, a boy developing a better ear for parental requests...he now picks up his blocks routinely and puts them away neatly after you ask him for the sixth time

THE BAD NEWS   Lookout for Deaf-Boy Teen, a miscreant stuck in an opium den of video games, glued to the screen, available and responding to parental communication only when you enlist the aid of a cattle prod

THE GOOD NEWS   Observe your Toddlerette take a relaxing, end-of-the-day bubble bath, making her squeaky-clean, freshly-jammied, and ready for Daddy's bedtime story

THE BAD NEWS   Observe your Teen Miss occupy the bathroom for three hours, spreading toiletries and cosmetics from ceiling to floor before yelling, "See ya!" and whirling out the door for her date with *Mr. Wonderful*

⌐   ⌐   ⌐   ⌐   ⌐

Toddlers and Teens,
Alike and Likeable (*?*)

I agree it's a mysterious link, but somehow your cute, cuddly toddler has teen blood in him. (Some would say it's *Type Werewolf*.) Perhaps it's because the teenage years and the toddler years are what your grandmother used to call, Awkward Times. Mmmmm. Like most grandmas, she hit the bullseye with understated wisdom.

Awkward Times indeed.

As we examined in the Good News-Bad News scenarios, both toddler times and teen times are about incredible change, sometimes a violent spasm, sometimes a beautiful epiphany. The issues are often serious in both age slots, but the point worth making here is that you, perceptive sire that you are, can learn from your toddler mistakes. Then, if you remember them well, after gliding through ages four through 12, you can apply your *toddler-education* to your upcoming *teen defense*.

Think of your toddler in teen terms. The essence of the toddler-teen connection is that both parties are desperately seeking independence from their cruel and dictatorial parents. Yet both are as attached as bubble gum to the sole of your shoe.

The toddler clings to you physically...ripping head, arm and leg hair from you when you attempt to dislodge the little gremlin from his stranglehold. Come adolescence, he or she will still be emotionally hitched to his parental units, only you won't find him or her the least bit huggable. Affection is way too uncool at this point. Peer pressure will forbid any direct display of it. So enjoy the bear cub hugs and sloppy kisses while you can.

While your toddler (momentarily) worships you, as a teen she will merely tolerate you. Yet her drive for independence is equally fierce at both stages. And rest assured, there will be times when her drive for freedom will drive you utterly mad. The toddler rebels against being a baby. The teen rebels against being a child.

Either way, you've got a *hellion* bent on *rebellion*.

Remember when you were a very little boy and someone asked you what you wanted to be when you grow up? Like most of us, you probably said "fireman" or "policeman." Well, now that you have a toddler, you get to be both. When Mommy's away or needs your help, the better you patrol your toddler beat—the better you play policeman—the less rescues you have to make as fireman.

Toddlers need to be watched closely. They do best with structure, organization, and direction...all in a loving, hands-on approach. Guess what? Teens are exactly the same.

Though you're watching closely, that's not to say you want to intervene constantly. Watch, guide, but don't confront continuously. With toddlers, you'll be a happier dad if you pick absolute battles sparingly. Otherwise, you'll be battling all day, every day. That's right. It works the same way with teens.

All the while you're dealing with the rebellion, earning your stripes as Pop the Cop, it helps if you keep reminding yourself one essential fact. However unruly, uncouth, or unfathomable your toddler or teen is...this time, this phase, this age will pass. I know. On a classically *bad* child care day, one that is both disgusting and unrewarding, the "long-term" "it-shall-pass" view brings little comfort.

But it's still true.

⌐   ⌐   ⌐   ⌐   ⌐

By now you've undoubtedly witnessed the worst your toddler has to offer. (Let's hope so, anyway!) But don't fret, he's got plenty of bad left in him. Enough to carry a healthy surplus of evil into his teen years and never run out.

More than anything it's this overwhelming NEGATIVE attitude that ties toddlers and teens together. Negativity is positively the hallmark trait of both ages. In other words, *Defiance* is the toddler-teen's calling card and the only word inscribed on the card is a big, fat NO!

But that's something you already know.

You already know many of the mannerisms your toddler will magically clone as a teen. You've beheld many of the common (bad) habits that mark the two groups. It's time now to examine the subtle differences that make caring for a teen or toddler the unadulterated nightmare that it is.

[187]

The Toddler-Teen Comparison Chart

	Toddler	Teen
Size	Smaller	Larger
Speed	Quick, except when it's time to eat, nap, bathe, potty or travel	Slow, except when playing sports. Exceptionally slow when work is involved
Shape	Dwarfish, oversized head, short legs, pudgy knees, puffy tummy, fat hands, chubby cheeks; a few otherwise here and there	Infinitely variable, always shifting... tiny, tall, thin, wide, long, lean, mini, immense
Voice	Loud, demanding— much screaming and crying, babbles, speaks mainly in monosyllables	Quiet, indifferent, changing—often cracks, speaks in monosyllables
Diet (free-range)	Candy, ice cream, cake, soda, cookies, insects, anything but vegetables	Pizza, candy, ice cream, cake, soda, tacos, anything but vegetables
Personality	The very definition of bipolar...your choice, either totally energized or asleep	Like a viper dozing in the desert, lazy, colorful and intriguing left unprovoked under its rock

	Toddler	Teen
Likes	Mommy, Grandma, tantrums, toys, blankie, thumb, any type of instant gratification	Self, sleep, opposite sex, pizza, movies, loud music, any/all instant gratification
Dislikes	Naps, potty, manners, sharing, doctors, rectal thermometers	School, homework, work, chores, parents, report cards
Hygiene	Will allow you to wipe hiney and suction boogies out of nose; prefers to wear poop-filled diaper for days	Showers forever or never at all, will pop zits for hours; prefers to wear the same jeans for days
Catch Phrase	*"Don't Wanna!"*	*"Leave Me Alone!"*
View of Family	Useful for cleaning up after me, bringing me gifts and praising me	Should all get lost, the sooner the better, except for cleaning up after me
Quirks	Caught in the right mood, will sit still for stories, lullabies, being held, hugs, kisses and cuddles	Approached quietly, will allow parent to enter room & talk— no touching allowed
Big Feat	Cleaning plate of squash; making poo-poo in potty; sharing doll with friend	Yes, finding shoes to fit his or her (canoe-size) feet

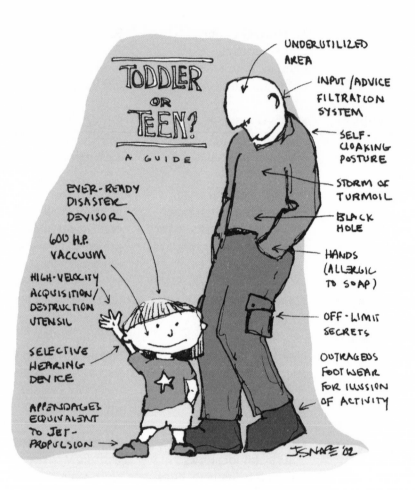

*Wanna Bet? A Wilder Pair of Jokers
You've Never Met*

Toddler-Teen Tactics: Fatherly Tips for Fighting a Losing Battle

One of life's great lessons is how to be a gracious loser. Believe me, I agree with you—winning is a lot more fun. The thing is, it's easy to be a winner. Losing, conversely, eats at the competitive male spirit and makes us rage against fate. Still, losing tests your character. It makes you work harder to put in a better performance the next time around.

Even if you've had the worst dad-day ever trying to care for your two- to four-year-old, take comfort in this chapter's message. No matter how bad it seems, remember things are going to get worse in eight to 10 years. Enjoy your toddler now! When she jumps on the adolescent train down the line, you'll wish you had your devilish, doe-eyed toddler-girl back.

In the meantime, here are a few parting tips that may boost your fathering success on both sides of the toddler-teen fence (*but please, don't count on it*).

—Go easy on coming down hard. Stay flexible. If you opt to be the super-dictator, Adolf, you're courting disappointment

—Let them have some independence, within reason. That's what they yearn for, and they're going to get it (you sincerely hope) sooner or later, regardless of your role

—Make their environment safe, but don't structure their world so rigidly that there is no room for an occasional mistake. Everyone learns from mistakes

—Keep your cool. You can't afford to have a tantrum every time your toddler does—and no one wants to see you if you did. A teen's looking for you to lose your temper, so don't

—Love them while they're little. They're easier to hug, easier to handle (most of the time) and easier to make happy (a lot of the time). Start now and keep it going

—Talk to her like she's big people. Communicate one-on-one. Stow the patronizing, little-people voice...she'll respect you more when she really is big

—Limit TV and video games as much as you can

—Give her your time, your patience, your wisdom. But don't spoil her with every material object in the world just because you love her

⌐   ⌐   ⌐   ⌐   ⌐

Okay. Taking care of toddlers and/or teens can be serious business, but that's about enough for one book. You can get bushels of certified serious advice from a bunch of other folks—and trust me, they can't wait to give it to you. Not only that, but you and I have plenty of time to be serious, like, for example, the rest of our lives.

For now, and for the rest of this book, let's you and I step away from the dreary, teary, grim and gloomy, and stick to the sunny, funny side of the street.

Chapter ten

Stammer, Clamor, Chatter and Charge

With Flag Unfurled, Your Mumbling,
Tumbling Tyke Takes On the World

> *The line it is drawn*
> *The curse it is cast*
> *The slow one now*
> *Will later be fast*
> *As the present now*
> *Will later be past*
> *The order is*
> *Rapidly fadin'.*
> *And the first one now*
> *Will later be last*
> *For the times they are a-changin'.*

> —Bob Dylan

Remember when we couldn't wait for our cute babies to learn how to walk and talk? Is it too late to start a Back to the Womb movement?

Now, we swerve our heads and gaze (aghast) across the room as our growing toddler flashes past like an untracked, targetless cruise missile...a screaming meteorite endangering every earthly inhabitant in its deadly crash path. As wise and faithful father-figures who have spawned these rumbling, rambling creatures, we stand tall and look down from our figurative paternal towers, expressions mixed with awe and disbelief. Who and/or what is this *wild thing*?

'Round and 'round and 'round she goes. Where she stops? Nobody knows.

Run for Your Life—Toddler on the Loose

Inside or out, home or away, your world is a carnival of unexpected sights and sounds. Around the age of three, every toddler becomes a crazed daredevil in perpetual stunt-mode. His or her motor is revved up and the gas pedal is floored. He or she shifts gears on the fly, without a thought, a care, or a prayer..off the road, over the cliff, into the canyon.

You watch, Pop-eyed, from the family room doorway or the playground bench, an eyewitness to a chronic car wreck, the endless crash unfolding before you. Scary. Bizarre. Destructive. Fascinating. You're a man in a trance hypnotized by a blur in poopy pants.

Just remember. You can be a dad wrapped up in a daze, but you're still the guy in charge while your wife's away. So get in shape. Keep up. Think fast. Step quicker. And if all else fails, get a good list of excuses together for when Mommy returns.

I know. Your toddler's a fascinating show, but you can't simply be an amused spectator, you have to stay in touch with the chaos. At times like these, you want to be a man taking the field and butting heads with the bedlam. For example...

He runs. He wrestles. He roars. He hops. He falls. He stops. He crawls on his belly like a reptile.

She shouts. She jumps. She kicks. She bounces. She sticks. She butts her head into the sofa like a billygoat.

Zoom! He whizzes by the merry-go-round and climbs to the top of the slide. He plunges down the ramp, stomps in the dirt, springs to the swing with a savage whoop. He falls belly-first on the strap and burps like a pig.

Whoa! She gallops past the jungle gym like a stampeding pony. She skids and stops, leaps to the gym and hooks her arm on a bar. She hangs like a monkey and chomps a make-believe banana in her other hand. She flops to the ground and cackles like a hyena.

If you're able to oversee several hours of commotion like the above, avoiding cracked skulls, broken limbs, bitten tongues and punctured eyeballs, then you deserve credit as a superior parent. Of course you won't get any credit, because parents only get credit when things go wrong. Worse still, as father caregivers and brothers-in-arms, we occupy a notch on the parenting totem pole just a tad below that of Big Chief Mommy.

So, as proposed earlier, while you're relaxing in your teepee easy chair, and your toddler's busy performing heap

[195]

big war dances on your ottoman, better start putting together a foolproof list of alibis in case your wife gets trigger-happy and starts spraying questions all over the place.

Upon her return, if she senses something astray, even the slightest damage to toddler or domicile, you'd best be ready to duel, quick-on-the-draw and sure-of-aim. Trust me. Keep your excuses close to your side, like bullets in your belt, lined up and ready to fire. Otherwise you're a dead man.

The (not-so) Brave Father's
Top 10 Roundup
of Toddler-Care Excuses

10.	Bruise on his forehead? What bruise? We did head bobs in the fingerpaint, that's all.

9.	So what if the car seat's turned sideways in the back of the van—it's still buckled, I can assure you. No, I didn't hear any muffled cries from the garage. But have you seen Junior since he and I got back from the store?

8.	Yes, I know his mother said Bobby went home crying. Becky shared her sandbox toys with him, too...she just didn't realize the bucket was filled with sand when she placed it upside-down on his head. I'm sure.

7.	Why, exactly, did his t-shirt shrink to the size of a doilie? Well, why don't they make microwaves with a permanent-press cycle?

6.   I don't care what Mrs. Katz said. The trip to the park went fine. What father would sit in a wagon reading the paper, yelling at his son to "pull harder, or else?"

5.   Of course the blue fish from the aquarium make for sick-looking sushi. I thought when he asked to "play chef," he meant a *make-believe* dinner.

4.   Honey, I've learned my lesson this time. No more play dough soccer using the open china cabinet as a net.

3.   Claire kept talking about baking cookies. Only I didn't notice the missing Duplo pieces till I smelled the oven and saw the colorful goo ooze out the door.

2.   What, Dear? The keyboard shelf on your computer desk is stuck again? Well, that solves the mystery about Jenny's peanut butter & jelly sandwich, thank goodness.

1.   Smell? Bathroom flood? Poop art on the wall? Yes! Yes! Yes! You never told me that disposable doesn't mean flushable, that's why.

⌐   ⌐   ⌐   ⌐   ⌐

Toddler-Actions Speak Louder than Words—or as one Dad cried, "Stop! I'm Deaf Already"

When your toddler passes 36 months and cruises into latter-day toddlerhood, you would think your paternal care worries would ease up a scrap or two. Not so, mon frére. The anguish just shifts a millimeter or two toward the larger end of the ruler. You might not be sweating the small stuff as much, but don't worry, you'll have plenty of macro-frights to weigh on your mind and keep your manly stress-levels peaking.

Along with Saint Vitus Toddler-itis crashing through your home indoors and out, you'll have a new set of sonic concerns to strike fear into your ears.

Your average 3-year-old is a din of destruction, a drum-thumping tympani of sound, a blasting racket of infinite noise turned permanently to Volume 10. Test the clamor for yourself. Go out to a popular chain eatery, just the two of you. Pin your elder toddler down in the booth for five minutes and listen. You'll see. And hear. In a crowded room, one 40-month-old is louder than 200 adults—easy.

Often, the sounds coming from your toddler's body will be more animal-like than human. This is normal. Learn to enjoy the weird noises and festive atmosphere of constant locomotion. We're talking about random grunts and growls, groans and grumbles. All matched by physical contortions, all around the booth opposite you. Unleashed, your todd will loudly scooch and slither, scrunch and pounce, then leap and bounce. Lower your eyes for two seconds, she'll be three booths down, whooping it up with a trio of senior citizens, helping them clean their fajita plates—faster than they have in years.

At this age, our toddlers demand our attention 24-hours a day, home or away. And while we're at it, we dads should give up trying to figure out their next move or verbal thought pattern. At a given moment, we may think the little gremlins are sweet and cuddly or monstrous and untouchable. And we can swell our brains all we like over the scientific where and why of our loved ones' boisterous, unsound behavior. But we need to remember one thing.

The Toddler Nation couldn't care less about our silly grown-up analyses and conclusions.

Still, witnessing your wunderkind's exploding vocabulary can be disquieting (surreal too), sort of like hearing a catfight in a faraway alley or listening to the faint thump of the landing gear coming out from the belly of the plane below you. You hear it, but you wonder if what you heard is *real*.

Real or not, decipherable or baffling, he babbles dozens of syllables per minute, talking to you, household pets, toys, imaginary friends and himself. He goes from articulating dozens of words at age two to hundreds of words and multiple-word phrases at age four. What? All of the words don't make sense to you? You can't understand half of what she's saying? Don't worry. She understands, and she's understanding more by the hour, and that's what counts.

In your role as smooth-talking, silver-tongued sire, all you need to do is be alert to the following linguistic discovery.

[199]

What's the Good Word?
The Ancient Toddler Tongue

That's right. Your delivery of Father-Toddler care is forever a defining moment in your saga of adult-male accomplishments. So don't shy away now just because your child's verbal onslaught raises the hair on the back of your neck. Instead, keep to the shadows, and listen intently to the secret language that every toddler deploys. It's an ancient tongue only little people use and understand. Learning a few choice definitions now could help boost your legacy as a well-defined dad.

In other words, take heed of these freshly-interpreted, common utterings as defined by the Ancient-Toddler Tongue.

"Uh-Oh"   means I've already flushed the toilet and whatever went down, is down forever

"Huh?"   means I know you've said one or the other 82 times today, but I would still like to know what, exactly, is the difference between "Stop it!" and "No!"

"Gimme!"   means get your slimy hands off my possession and return it NOW because it ain't yours and I ain't sharing

"No!"   the most-used word in the Toddler Tongue, means "Stupid Parent, it doesn't matter what you say or do, what you want to happen is not happening anytime soon"

"Go!"   means get out of my sight, get out of my life, and don't come back anytime soon

"Pweeze" means that is something I desire very much... so much that I am willing to humble myself by using one of those stupid *magic words* you keep forcing on me

"Tank oooh" means against my better judgment, I'll use another *magic word*—just keep the cookies coming

"Ow!" means you better get the Band-Aid box in a hurry cause this scrape on my knee is ten time worse than it looks, trust me

"Bye-Bye" means you bore me to death and I'm certainly glad to be leaving, but as you watch me depart be sure to observe how cute I am waving goodbye to you

"Mine!" means I know this belongs to the other toddler, but it looks interesting and I'm going to snatch it NOW

"Want Dat" means I understand this object lives on the retail shelf, and we don't need it, but you'll save yourself a lot of trouble if you put it in the cart NOW

"See" means I knew that was going to break into a million pieces...why don't you stop me next time?

"Me" means the center of the universe, the object of all affection, the most important individual in the history of the world, the shining light that all dimmer lights revolve around

"Ugh" means get those disgusting-looking vegetables off my plate and out of my sight because they're not passing my lips, and you'd best not kid yourself about it now or ever

[201]

The Greatest Lies of Toddlerhood

They may have totally self-centered agendas and a specialized vocabulary for getting their way, but a least your average toddler will talk to you straight about what's on his or her mind. A toddler is basically an honest little devil at heart. Dangerously self-absorbed, but still honest.

On the other hand, the adults surrounding you and your toddler on your typical pappy-care day love to lie to you. They will tell you big, fat lies for as long as you will listen. They tell you lies and then they laugh at you behind your back. So be on your daddy-toes for these classic falsehoods:

1) "Oh, nonsense. Your living room doesn't look *that* bad."

2) "I had the same trouble toilet-training my son. It can't be helped and there's nothing to be embarrassed about in public."

3) "Don't worry. My daughter didn't talk till she was three."

4) "If your wife told you to buy that brand of oatmeal, that's what you should get."

5) "You go ahead. Someone will mop that up later."

6) "Isn't she beautiful! She looks just like you."

7) "Your son is so well-mannered at the table."

8) "It's okay. I've had to clean up worse messes, lots of times."

9) "That's not picky. That's normal."

[202]

10) "I bet he's a little angel...most of the time."

11) "Our dog's a good sport. She doesn't mind."

12) "No problem. We're glad you came over to visit."

13) "Your daughter was a joy to have at our playdate. We'll call you about setting up another one."

14) "I wish my husband would help out like you do."

15) "Really. I've seen more violent tantrums."

16) "We wouldn't think about pressing charges over a little incident like that."

⌐　　⌐　　⌐　　⌐　　⌐

The Last Rights of Toddlerhood

When your toddler's preschool-ready, will you be ready to see her go? Will you smile to bid toddlerhood adieu? Yes or no? Are these questions fair, dear father? Yes. Or maybe no.

I know this. Looking too far ahead into our children's lives is dangerous business. Each stage of father-parenting is all-consuming and it's difficult to see what lies next. Besides, our precious offspring give us little warning about shifting tides as they shoot up the growth chart. Better to try to do the right father-thing every day, and hope to remember the lesson when we do wrong.

In toddler-daddying, there are rights and wrongs, ups and downs, good days and bad. So if you're a father who's into perfectionism...a guy who wants to get everything right every time, I have unfortunate news for you. There are toddler mishaps, yea, even disasters that you won't be able to *affect*, let alone *change*. Ease up trying to be perfect. Just try to give your toddler the best care you can give, day-to-day.

Then, when things go really bad...like the day when the washing machine and toilet overflow at once...the same day the dining room wall gets a crayon mural...the day your wife comes home with the fire truck still sitting in the drive... the day before your neighbor sticks a FOR SALE sign in your lawn as a hint...that infamous day when you and your child have to visit the emergency room *twice* (the Fire Chief drove the second time)...you'll be able to throw up your hands, look your wife in the eye and say, "I did my best, honey. Obviously, it wasn't good enough. But there's always tomorrow. *Isn't there?*"

Your wife may be Mommy on the Warpath, especially after she sees your toddler's bandages, a woman who wants your scalp and a piece of your hide. But if you're truthful and contrite, and you let her compose herself, she'll probably shake her head and say something like, "Listen, mister. I know first-hand how tough taking care of toddlers can be. But you're right. tomorrow is another day.

"That's why I'm taking the day off, so we can tackle this toddler-care thing together—at least for the next 36 hours."

[204]

POP'S TOP 40

TODDLERIFIC

HITS

*A weird and wonderful list of musical treasures
designed to charm your toddler into
lobotomy-like bliss*

⌐   ⌐   ⌐   ⌐   ⌐   ⌐   ⌐

Shakespeare once said, "Here we will sit and let the sounds of music Creep in our ears...." and "The man that hath no music in himself, Nor is not moved with concord of sweet sounds, Is fit for treasons, stratagems, and spoils."

Of course, what the old bard was really talking about was a devastating toddler-care experience which nearly cost the man his literary touch. After four months of wifely-plotted

[205]

daily toddler-custody in a small cottage down the street from his grammar school, poor Shake's brain when blank. Little wonder—at one time he oversaw the double-trouble of twin toddlers! Luckily for us, the poet from Stratford-upon-Avon eventually translated his pain into a work of art entitled *The Merchant of Venice.*

The point is, take it from old Will. The only way he stayed sane is by plucking a lute and singing the latest Elizabethan tunes for his eager toddler-audience. He discovered what we modern dads know for fact. That is, music and toddlers go together like ham and eggs. And the hammier it is, the more they like it.

So throw another log on the fire, stock your iPod, DVD, CD or MP3 player with a tasty menu of mixable, matchable melodies. Then ham it up like two merry minstrels on a tour of tunesville.

When things look bleak and you're ready to shriek... when the bough breaks, your cranium aches, and you've come up suddenly with a bad case of the toddler-care shakes...then it's time to dish up a savory entree of delightful ditties designed to parallel any (warped) toddler frame of mind.

Browse each chapter heading and discover song titles which add musical luster to your current toddler situation. If you have time, look up the lyrics on the Internet. Then you can let it all hang out. Polish the floor, punch up a groovy tune, waltz into the family room and get ready to twist and shout. Go on, cut the rug and raise a little cane. The two of you can frolic like fools till Mommy gets home again.

[206]

Pop and Todd's Top 40 Toddlerific Hits

Prologue
Welcome to the Terrible Twos

Chapter One
Too Pooped to Pop

Chapter Two
The Name of the Game is "Pack Man"

Chapter Three
The Toddler Table: Serving Whine
with Every Meal

11) *Mashed Potato Time* .... Dee Dee Sharp
12) *Eat a Peach* (album) .... Allman Brothers Band
13) *Sugar, Sugar*........................... The Archies
14) *I Ain't Gonna Eat Out My Heart Anymore*. . The Rascals

Chapter Four
Temper Tantrum: The Toddler National Anthem

15) *Whole Lotta Shakin' Going On* .... Jerry Lee Lewis
16) *Voodoo Child* .... Jimi Hendrix
17) *Tell Her No*........................... The Zombies

Chapter Five
How Not to be a Weenie When It's Time to Wean

15) *You and Me & the Bottle Makes Three (Tonight)*
.... Big Bad Voodoo Daddy
19) *Squeeze Box*............................ The Who
20) *Cold Turkey*......................... John Lennon

Chapter Six
A Snotty Attitude Toward the Common Cold

21) *Bad Case of Loving You (Doctor, Doctor)*. Robert Palmer

22) *The Witch Doctor* . . . David Seville & The Chipmunks

23) *Fever* . . . . Peggy Lee

Chapter Seven
Lullabies, Cries and Bloodshot Zombie Eyes

24) *Here Come those Tears Again*. . . . . Jackson Browne

25) *The Crying Game*. . . . . Boy George

26) *The Sleeping Beauty* . . . . Tchaikovsky

27) *There's a Kind of Hush* . . . . Herman's Hermits

28) *Semper Fidelis* . . . . John Philip Sousa

Chapter Eight
Toilet Training Builds a Pant-Load of Trust

29) *Go Now* . . . . The Moody Blues

30) *Love Stinks*. . . . . J. Geils Band

31) *Takin' Care of Business* . . . Bachman-Turner Overdrive

32) *Go Your Own Way* . . . . Fleetwood Mac

33) *Hot Pants*. . . . . James Brown

Chapter Nine
Toddlers Are Like Teens Only Smaller

Chapter Ten
Clamor, Stammer, Chatter and Charge

♩   ♩   ♩   ♩   ♩

A Few Thank-Yous

Proving you're not a one-hit wonder takes time. It also takes the caring presence and counsel of a host of people, not to mention their time. You know who you are, but you may not realize how much you really helped. Thanks from the heart.

Susan, Meghan and Shannon, knowing you care about my success inspires me to be a better writer. I keep working on it, and I do humbly thank you for your deep-well of tolerance. I think we're getting there.

Mom, I wish so much again that you could be here and see this second book. So much of your humor is in it. Dad, you too, I know you would be proud of its potential.

Jason Snape, I feel lucky to have found you... you're a talented illustrator and a trusty ally as well. This book surely wouldn't be as good as it is without you. For graphics (and general) advice, I'm also indebted to Cynthia Webb, Ed Cahill, Karen Shelnutt, David Bridges and Ben Broome.

Thanks to the folks at IPG...Mary Rowles, Susan Sewall, Jason Maynard, Mark Voigt, Mark Suchomel, Chad Atwood, Kristen Aldorisio and all. A special thanks to USA Baby's Jacque Sternquist, and all USA Baby store owners, especially Sheryl and Richard Cohen, for supporting Clearing Skies Press.

For encouragement that sticks with you, I want to thank John McClaugherty and Bob Cramer (as always), as well as Mike Gleason, Greg Swayne and Stuart Epley. To my sisters-in-law, Meg, Jane and especially Kathy (thanks!); and to brothers-in-law Cray, Dan, David, and Pat —let's get up to the Cabin *soon* and do a little trout-fishing.